Kotaro

The Spirit of Wind and one of the twelve supreme-level spirits. Inhabits the body of a sacred beast from the Nation of the Spirit King. He adores Ruri and is always by her side like a faithful dog.

Rin

The Spirit of Water and one of the twelve supreme-level spirits. She takes a liking to Ruri and accompanies her after Ruri gives her a name.

Jade

The young and wise ruler of the Nation of the Dragon King. Takes Ruri, a Beloved, into his care and dotes on her. In contrast to his cool and suave demeanor, he has a soft spot for all things cute and cuddly. He gives Ruri his dragonheart as proof that she's his mate, and they are now husband and wife.

Ruri Morikawa

A girl summoned to an alternate world after getting wrapped up in her childhood "friend's" nonsense. She is a Beloved, a person whose mana is especially attractive to spirits. By putting on a special bracelet, she can transform into a white cat. She marries Jade, but she finds his doting behavior slightly overbearing.

Character Introductions

THE WHITE CAT'S REVENGE AS PLOTTED FROM THE DRAGON KING'S LAP: VOLUME 6

by: KUREHA
Illustrations by Yamigo
Translated by David Evelyn
Edited by Suzanne Seals
Layout by Cheree Smith
English Print Cover by Kai Kyou

First published in Japan in 2021 by Frontier Works Inc.
Publication rights for this English edition arranged through Frontier Works Inc., Tokyo
English translation © 2022 J-Novel Club LLC

Managing Director: Samuel Pinansky
Light Novel Line Manager: Chi Tran
Managing Editor: Jan Mitsuko Cash
Managing Translator: Kristi Fernandez
QA Manager: Hannah N. Carter
Marketing Manager: Stephanie Hii
Project Manager: Nikki Lapshinoff

ISBN: 978-1-7183-2044-4
Printed in Korea
First Printing: January 2023
10 9 8 7 6 5 4 3 2 1

Contents

Contents

 **Prologue**

A chalk-white castle floated atop a lake. It was the Nation of the Spirit King's royal castle, where the Spirit King dwelled. It was also where the Spirit of Trees, a supreme-level spirit with the body of a great tree, resided. The great tree had been there ever since the founding of the nation, reaching toward the heavens and watching over the kingdom.

The nation's people were spirit-religious, meaning they worshipped the spirits—albeit not as fervently as the Nation of the Beast King. Because of this, they had not seen strife or conflict for a long time. In fact, the Nation of the Spirit King had a long history. It was the oldest kingdom in the world with the oldest surviving records. The Spirit King, Awain, had supported the nation as its ruler since its inception.

Awain had eyes as blue as the deepest sea and shoulder-length blueish silver hair. Unfortunately, something about his face just looked vicious, so much so that it would make any child cry. Despite that, he was tall and slender and—if you looked hard enough at his face without flinching—handsome, so it was a shame that his general look wound up offsetting everything else. He had a high approval rating among the nation's people, though, regardless of his appearance.

Contrary to his countenance, Awain was an extremely sensitive soul. People would often catch him sulking in private because despite his love for children, they were terrified of him. It was similar to how Jade would pout when a fluffy little animal ran away from him.

Awain belonged to a race called qilins. They were highly intelligent, and their mana was stronger than that of a dragonkin. Qilins had perpetual youth, so Awain appeared to be in his mid-thirties, despite being the oldest king of the oldest nation in the world. Sadly, he was the only pure-blooded qilin left in the world. Qilins had difficulty producing offspring, which was why their numbers were dwindling.

Awain did have a son—Lapis, who was also a Beloved—but Lapis hadn't inherited any of the qilin qualities. Awain had absolutely no intention of taking another spouse either, because he was still in love with his deceased wife. Consequently, the qilin race would most likely die out with him.

Awain himself didn't care much about that. He was more concerned with his nation's present and future. However, what claimed all his attention right now was a sacred beast.

"Have you found the culprit yet?" Awain asked the people in his office, who were all looking pensive.

"No, sire. Our apologies. We split our forces to investigate, but we still haven't found anything."

"I see."

Awain sighed, his brow tensing so hard that the ensuing wrinkles made his already vicious-looking face appear downright ferocious. Fortunately, he was surrounded by his trusted aides and vassals, all of whom were immune to Awain's lethal facial expression. None of them were fazed by the display. They just continued with their discussion.

Some time ago, the Nation of the Spirit King's sacred beast died from poisoning. It had still been a cub, so its childlike curiosity and lack of awareness had probably contributed to the incident. It had eaten the food it was given without any sense of danger.

Although the cub had lost its life, the supreme-level Spirit of Wind had asked to use its physical body for some reason or another.

No one had objected, stating that it was better than leaving the corpse as it was. The supreme-level Spirit of Trees, the guardian of the nation, had approved it as well.

A mere mortal could never interfere in the spirits' wishes to begin with, and Awain wasn't the only one glad it had worked out that way. There was a secret about sacred beasts known by only a select handful of people. When a sacred beast died, their body produced a certain substance. That substance could be used to make a very powerful elixir, and there was even a time far in the past when they were hunted solely for that reason.

Awain and the Spirit of Trees had helped safeguard these animals since the founding of the nation. In order to protect them, they'd declared that the beasts were important to the nation—they were sacred. Since the sacred beasts were now behind the castle walls and there were limited chances to see them, knowledge of the elixir was eventually lost to time. And thanks to the castle's protection, their population had stopped decreasing, though they were still on the brink of extinction due to their low fertility rates.

Never before had anyone been foolish enough to commit a crime under the watchful eye of the Spirit of Trees…and yet it had happened. Awain was utterly shocked that a cub in his protection had been killed, and so was everyone else who worked in the castle. The person who'd poisoned the cub was one of its regular caretakers—a very diligent and hardworking individual. No one had suspected that he would commit such a heinous act. Even after they'd learned of their acquaintance's guilt, those who knew him were unanimous in their disbelief.

No one knew why the caretaker had poisoned the cub in the first place. Before anyone could find out, the caretaker had suspiciously died in his jail cell. Judging from the erratic scratch marks he'd left on his own chest, it was clear that he'd been poisoned.

They had thoroughly inspected his belongings before he was placed in his cell and had found nothing, so it was suspected that the poison had been brought in from elsewhere.

Awain suspected that the caretaker's murder was a cover-up, but that was merely his intuition speaking. He did know that there had to be a mastermind behind the poisoning. Although they hadn't been able to identify why someone had killed the cub, Awain feared that it was to obtain the special substance from the sacred beast's corpse. However, only a select group of people within the nation knew of that secret, and all were from families who'd served the Nation of the Spirit King since times of old. Awain didn't want to doubt any of them, but he had to fulfill his kingly duties and get to the bottom of this matter.

Awain had asked an especially trustworthy aide in his court to conduct a top secret investigation, but they hadn't been able to identify the mastermind or discover the reason behind the attack. With nothing to go on, Awain had contemplated every possibility from every angle, but he still hadn't come up with any other plausible reason aside from the special substance.

Ever since the incident, Awain had tightened the security around the sacred beasts more than ever. He was praying that there wouldn't be another casualty, but that would require identifying the ringleader.

"Still, Your Majesty, we cannot focus our attention on this alone," said Awain's aide.

"Yes, I am well aware."

The incident was indeed important, but no matter how peaceful the Nation of the Spirit King was, it wasn't without its issues. Maintaining a nation that had been around for eons was a difficult task. As Spirit King, Awain had more than just one task to attend to. He couldn't get hung up solely on the killing of a sacred beast.

"There is also the issue with the Nation of Iolite," said the aide.

"Yes, I remember. Oh, my aching head," Awain complained, massaging his temple.

The Nation of Iolite was located not far from the Nation of the Spirit King, but a neighboring nation had wiped it out a few years ago. They had executed every member of its royal family and absorbed the country, erasing it off the map.

That much was a common occurrence, so it wasn't an issue. The Nation of the Spirit King wouldn't take sides unless an allied nation was involved. Part of their pact with the Spirit of Trees was that they wouldn't stick their neck out unnecessarily. Because of that, the Nation of the Spirit King had remained exclusively spectators.

However, Awain had heard that the nation that absorbed Iolite imposed excessively heavy taxes on its former people, thereby oppressing them. As a result, those who couldn't pay became thieves who haunted the roads leading to the Nation of the Spirit King. Some became pirates, attacking the Nation of the Spirit King's ships and carrying out other nefarious acts. It was starting to directly affect the country, so the Nation of the Spirit King could no longer sit on the sidelines.

"There's a meeting of the Alliance of Four Nations coming up soon," Awain said, "but there is a mound of issues to attend to." He preferred to cast everything aside and run away, but his serious and diligent nature wouldn't let him.

"Not only will Celestine of the Nation of the Beast King be attending, but also the Beloved of the Nation of the Dragon King. We shall need to be more vigilant than usual," commented the aide.

Awain nodded. "The Beloved of the Nation of the Dragon King has contracted three supreme-level spirits. Although highly unlikely, we must try not to earn their ire."

"Yes, about that. Will the supreme-level spirits also be attending?"

That was the court's biggest concern. Supreme-level spirits were sublime entities, and most people had gone their entire lives without seeing one. Once the court heard that Ruri had not only contracted several supreme-level spirits but had even subjugated them by giving them names, their surprise turned into speechlessness. They'd also heard that aside from the group of contracted spirits, several other supreme-level spirits were gathered in the Nation of the Dragon King. The power balance between the four nations was completely askew.

Fortunately, Ruri had visited the Nation of the Spirit King in the past, and from what they'd seen of her, she wasn't a bad person who would abuse her power. Actually, she'd left a favorable impression because of how she interacted with the spirits like friends.

Not everyone could be as casual around supreme-level spirits as Ruri, though. The people in the castle were used to interacting with the Spirit of Trees, but they hadn't learned how to deal with *multiple* supreme-level spirits. What if they were to accidentally upset any of those spirits? The mere thought of it was enough to give the aides stomachaches.

"According to the Spirit of Trees, she doesn't seem to be unreasonable," Awain assured them. "If the situation calls for it, the Spirit of Trees will intervene on our behalf, so don't fret."

"Yes, well, one can only hope, sire," the aide replied.

"Well, I wouldn't worry about it. Just act like you would normally. Also, see to it that the welcome party is in order."

"As you wish."

The aides exited the room, leaving Awain alone to peer out the window. He looked at the great tree that towered high into the sky.

"We must do something before there are more casualties. Should push come to shove, we might have to ask the Spirit of Trees for their assistance," Awain said aloud, but he wanted to avoid that option as much as possible.

Spirits wouldn't back anyone unless they were under contract with them. The Spirit of Trees had protected the nation, but that was because of their own personal feelings. They weren't necessarily siding with Awain or the Nation of the Spirit King. That was why, even with the sacred beast incident, Awain had only asked the Spirit of Trees for facts and reports and nothing else. But if things went any further, Awain would have no choice but to ask for the spirit's assistance.

"This is such a massive headache…"

Newlywed Life

Some time had passed since Ruri and Jade's wedding. After the ceremony, they'd taken a honeymoon trip to the Nation of the Spirit King to meet the Spirit of Trees. Despite the altercation she'd had with Lapis, the Nation of the Spirit King's Beloved, Ruri had enjoyed her honeymoon speaking with the Spirit of Trees and walking around the nation's royal capital.

Ever since she'd returned, Ruri had been living the newlywed life with Jade—an experience so sugary sweet that it made her want to shout it from the rooftops. But there were also the ubiquitous third wheels interrupting at every turn.

"Oh, Ruuuriii!"

Ruri heard the familiar elderly voice and rolled her eyes from atop Jade's lap, where she lay in cat form. She was dreading yet another day of this.

"Here we go again..."

Jade stroked Ruri's head as he sighed wearily.

"You're being far too loud, Agate."

Agate and the other elder vassals had arrived to visit the happy couple.

"How are you feeling, Ruri? About ready to have children?"

Agate's question was practically a daily routine at this point, and Ruri's patience was running extremely thin.

"*Oh. My.* God. *I keep telling you each and every day you ask, but there's no way I'll be 'ready' the day after you pose the* same darn question*!*"

Ruri's fur stood on end. It was clear how much Agate and the other elders had their hearts set on a royal baby, but they were being extremely insensitive.

The elders slumped in disappointment.

"Oh, bother. Still?"

"Don't you think you've been taking a little *too much* time?"

"Your Majesty, might I suggest that you dedicate more private time between you two?"

Ruri's face flushed, instantly running hot. This had gone past insensitivity and straight into sexual harassment.

"You are all well aware of how busy I've been with work. I won't be able to have any personal time with Ruri, so we can't tend to the deed right away," Jade replied nonchalantly.

"*Jade-sama!*"

Ruri trembled in shame, wondering if Jade was out of his mind to respond like that.

"Hm? What?" asked Jade.

His voice had turned almost syrupy, and the sudden sweetness eliminated any objections she had.

"*Urk, never mind...*"

"Oh? Okay."

As Jade petted her fluffy head, she simply buried her face in her paws and waited for Agate and the other elders to leave.

"In that case, we've no choice but to bump up the time you two can spend with one another," said one elder.

"Maybe we should get more people to help with the king's work?" said another.

"Let's hash out a plan, everyone!"

"Excellent!"

And just like that, the group came and went like a tornado. Ruri heaved a deep sigh and wondered how Agate and his posse could still be so very active at their age.

After a while, Jade put down his pen. Ruri suspected that he was taking a break and lifted her head, but Jade suddenly took off her bracelet and placed it atop his desk. Ruri reverted back to human form in the blink of an eye. Jade cradled her body and planted a light kiss on her lips. He stared lovingly at her as her cheeks flushed.

Jade always treated her carefully. It was almost like being wrapped in cotton. She occasionally had to deal with his dragonkin possessiveness, but she spent each day treasuring his love and the serene happiness it brought.

Jade wrapped his large hands around her cheeks and brought his lips to hers over and over, delivering kisses that were far deeper than the light pecks he'd started off with. It wasn't long before Ruri had her fill, but Jade showed no signs of stopping.

Jade would kiss Ruri like this at even the slightest repose. As he dealt with his kingly duties, he would keep Ruri by his side as much as possible. Then, once he decided he could take a break from his work, he would persistently kiss her for what seemed like forever.

Although Ruri was anxious that someone would suddenly come into the office, she didn't *dislike* Jade's advances. She usually let him have his way, despite her embarrassment. However, Jade was getting incessant, and he wouldn't let go once he'd started.

Ruri was nearing her limits. She put some power into her arms and wrenched herself away from Jade. She happened to see his disappointed face, but she couldn't let herself fall for it.

"I can't handle any more," Ruri said, pulling her face away as if it was her only recourse. She was panting heavily.

Jade, on the other hand, wasn't letting go, and she couldn't escape from his arms. She didn't really mind since she wasn't intending to escape anyway, but Jade's frequent physical intimacy drove her to twisting and shouting on occasion.

Ruri used to blush just from sitting on Jade's lap in human form, but Jade had smothered her with so much close contact that she didn't have the leeway to care every time it happened. Nevertheless, even though Ruri was more used to things now, she was still a beginner, and the constant, heavy touching was still too much for her to endure. She'd had no idea that Jade was such a compulsive kisser until she'd married him. Perhaps this was just how newlyweds were supposed to act, but Ruri couldn't keep up with Jade's pace.

"Um, Jade-sama, would you mind toning it down a little bit?" Ruri timidly suggested, fearing that she wouldn't be able to hold up if this went on. But Jade's icy stare made her quickly correct herself, and she added, "I-I mean, I'm not saying that I don't like it, but just a little!"

"If it doesn't bother you, then there should be no problem," Jade nonchalantly replied.

Ruri gave herself a mental pep talk, telling herself not to give in, and then tried to plead her case.

"No, I mean, I know what I said, but I won't be able to hold up if we do this every single day. Physically or mentally!"

Ruri was mainly concerned about the stress on her heart. She'd heard that a dragonkin's love for their mate was strong, but this was beyond her expectations. It was so bad as of late that he would get grumpy whenever she wasn't in eyeshot.

Ruri, being a human, had initially thought that it would settle down after a while, but she had severely underestimated dragonkin. The more days that passed, the worse Jade's possessiveness became. Ruri didn't necessarily feel inconvenienced since she'd originally been in cat form most of the time around Jade, but she did wish that he would keep in mind that she was a human and take it a little easier on her.

"But this is also for your sake too, Ruri."

"*How*?!" Ruri asked, not understanding what part of kissing was for her benefit.

"What, no one told you?"

"Told me what?" Ruri's eyes went wide. She hadn't expected there to be an actual reason.

"I thought that Agate or one of the others would have told you when they explained the marriage ceremony, but I venture they didn't tell you anything?"

"I have no idea what you're talking about, so no?"

"You were told that a dragonkin male can only have a child with the mate he gave his dragonheart to, right?"

"That I was."

Before the wedding, Agate had given Ruri a general rundown of the dragonkin marriage ceremony. Mates would swallow the dragonheart, thus making a contract to be spouses. If the marriage was between two dragonkin, both would exchange dragonhearts and swallow them, but other races could become a dragonkin spouse just fine by swallowing their mate's dragonheart. If the woman was a dragonkin and the man was of a different race, the man could hope for a child by swallowing her dragonheart. But if the man was the dragonkin, the woman *had* to swallow the dragonheart or she wouldn't be able to conceive. It was apparently necessary in order to raise as strong a dragonkin as possible within the mother's womb.

"Things don't simply end when you give your dragonheart to your mate," Jade explained. "Since the dragonheart is a foreign object, the dragonkin must send mana into the dragonheart and tune it in order to make sure it acclimates to the mate's body."

"Tune it?"

"Haven't you felt anything unusual when we kiss?"

"No, my mind is always so *overloaded* that I can't think of anything else," Ruri said, her expression serious.

Jade chuckled. "If that's the case, then try to sense my mana a little more," he said, bringing his face to hers and giving her a light peck.

Ruri focused her attention on their lips and felt something slightly warm and magical flowing into her from Jade. It was a comforting power that she recognized.

"I'm sure you felt something enter your body now, correct?" asked Jade.

"Yes, I did."

"That was my mana. Given how you've been acting, it seems you hadn't noticed that I've been streaming mana into you."

"Not in the slightest..." Ruri replied, chalking it up to her discomposure when they kissed.

"Unless I prepare and tune the dragonheart to your body by pouring mana into you, then you won't be able to have children."

"If that's the case, then why do Agate-san and the others keep coming to ask me every day? They should know that I can't have a child if I'm not ready yet."

"Agate's group isn't so much asking if you're personally ready for children, but more so if you are properly tuned. Also, once I tune my dragonheart to you, it will make your body stronger—not as strong as a dragonkin, but strong enough. It will prevent slight injuries or illness. Humans are a weak and frail race that soon dies from illness or injury. That is why Agate's group is so worried about you and asks whether you're in tune every day."

Ruri was shocked to hear that those incessantly annoying questions were out of concern for her. She felt bad that she'd assumed they were being a gang of harassing old codgers.

"So how long does it take to get in sync?" Ruri asked.

"Dragonkin usually take a honeymoon vacation after the wedding where they eat and sleep with their mate for a month," Jade replied.

"Grk! *That* long?" Ruri exclaimed, her face tensing into a grimace. Just hearing those words made her almost pass out.

"No, that is just between two dragonkin. It will take time for the dragonheart to adjust to a human like you—even *more* time."

"*Whaaa*?!"

"Also, it will probably take longer than that since I have my kingly duties to attend to. Though, considering that Agate's group is preparing something to alleviate that, I assume I'll be able to spend more time giving you my mana."

That essentially meant that a hailstorm of kisses—even more ferocious than now—would be sweeping over Ruri.

"Unghh…" Ruri groaned. She could no longer oppose it after hearing that there was a reason for this all. Still, she was relieved that things were over for today.

"By the way, you seem to have perked up considerably," Jade said with a daunting and *amorous* grin.

Noticing the look on his face, Ruri let out a voiceless cry and plotted her escape. But Jade quickly took her into his embrace, thwarting her attempts. She timidly looked up at him, and Jade gave her a beaming smile.

"The quicker we tune you up, the quicker you'll shut up Agate's group, you know?" Jade proclaimed, slowly drawing his face to Ruri's.

With no choice but to concede, Ruri closed her eyes. She endured yet another draining affair until Claus arrived at the office.

2 The Cuddle Ban

On the same day, Ruri was standing in the kitchen—without Jade. They'd been almost inseparable since they'd wed, so it was an unusual sight. But just because Jade wasn't by her side, it didn't mean that she was alone; Kotaro, Rin, and other lesser spirits were surrounding her.

Kotaro and Rin had said that they were unhappy she'd been spending more time with Jade and less with the spirits. They congratulated her on her marriage, but they were still upset. Not even Jade could ignore a massive gang of spirits all asking Ruri to give them attention as well, so he'd had to reluctantly let her go.

Ruri had decided to bake cookies for the spirits. It was the first time she'd hung out with them in a long while. Kotaro, Rin, and the others were ecstatic to have Ruri all to themselves. Kotaro, for example, was very excitedly wagging his tail. His canine loyalty was as steadfast as ever. Rin was also jovially flying circles around Ruri.

"*It's been so long since I've had your cookies, Ruri,*" said Kotaro. The scent coming from the oven made his nose twitch in delight.

"*Isn't that the truth?! Ruri has been spending all her time with the king as of late,*" Rin added.

"Hey, listen, I'm sorry. I'm really sorry," apologized Ruri. "I never thought that Jade-sama would get *that* clingy."

"*Dragonkin are very possessive of their mates, after all,*" stated Rin.

"Yeah, I've heard the stories before, but still…"

"*Some dragonkin mates can't handle their spouse's attachment and end up running away, so you should be careful, Ruri,*" Rin explained, clarifying that it wasn't a concern when both parties were dragonkin.

Ruri knew quite a bit about how attached a dragonkin could get because of the former Dragon King, Quartz. His extraordinary fixation on Seraphie, his mate, would probably be incomprehensible to a human being. It had even driven him to abdicate the throne and wander the world in search of her reincarnation.

"Well, you can warn me to be careful, but I don't know *what* to be careful of," retorted Ruri.

"*Just don't make him jealous,*" Rin suggested. "*Then again, the king is a rather reasonable dragonkin, so I doubt there's much to worry about. Besides, we'll be here for you if things get ugly!*"

The other spirits raised their hands in solidarity.

"*I'll help you escape~!*"

"*Me too!*"

"*Let's just beat 'em down!*"

"*Should we bury them?*"

"*We'll beat 'em to a pulp~!*"

All of the spirits started happily discussing how they would beat Jade black and blue.

Ruri scrambled to quash their discussion, saying, "I-I appreciate the sentiment, guys, but that *won't* be necessary."

It would be terrible if Jade suffered a surprise attack under Ruri's nose. The spirits' loyalty to a Beloved was frightening.

"*Ruri~! They're done~!*" called a fire spirit who'd been watching the oven.

"Right! On it!" replied Ruri.

She pulled the sheet pan out of the oven, revealing the beautiful golden brown cookies. They smelled delectable.

"They turned out nice!" Ruri remarked.

"*Wow! They're done!*"

"*They smell so good!*"

"*They turned out so well~!*"

Ruri moved the cookies from the pan to a plate, making sure to avoid getting burned, and let them cool a little. Then she picked up one and put it in her mouth. It was crispy and had just the right amount of sweetness.

"Mmm~! Oh yeah, nothing beats a cookie fresh out of the oven."

Rin shouted, "*Me too! Me too!*"

"*I also want one!*" exclaimed Kotaro.

Once Ruri gave both Rin and Kotaro a cookie each, they stuffed their cheeks. However, it seemed that one cookie wasn't nearly enough for Kotaro with his gigantic body. He stared at the pile sitting on the plate with sparkling eyes.

"Wait just a second," Ruri said, splitting the cookies into shares for Kotaro and Rin. Then she put the rest on a large plate.

The eagle-eyed Rin looked at it, asking, "*Ruri, what's that big pile for?*"

"I'm taking that to Lydia's for a tea party. I haven't seen her in a while either."

"*Yes, I'm sure Time will be pleased,*" Kotaro affirmed. He was interested in how Lydia was doing as well.

Since Lydia couldn't leave the pocket space, guests had to go there to see her. There was a limited number of people who could enter that space, though. Kotaro and the other spirits shared a unique spirit-only connection with Lydia, but they couldn't enter the space that she inhabited. As a result, Lydia was alone. She couldn't travel freely or meet others like the spirits on the outside, even with that connection. Ruri would ask why that was, but Lydia would only vaguely answer, "That's just how things work."

There was a lot that Ruri didn't know about spirits, even though they were always so close to her. As a human, Ruri couldn't even begin to understand. The only thing she could do was visit the pocket space on occasion and have tea parties with Lydia. Even if it was something as small and silly as that, it was still enjoyable for Lydia since she was forced to stay there. That was exactly why Ruri felt sorry for not visiting her sooner.

Ruri had prepared the tea and was about to go to Lydia's place, when Seraphie, Quartz's mate, suddenly popped up.

"Oh my, what are you doing, Ruri?" she asked.

"Oh, it's you, Seraphie-san. I was planning to have a tea party with Lydia in the pocket space, so I'm getting ready for it."

"Oh, that sounds fun. Care if I join you?"

Seraphie was a ghost. Before she died, she'd used sorcery to transfer her soul into a ring so that she could remain in the world of the living—all for Quartz's sake. Quartz hadn't known about her plan, though, and had buried the ring along with her remains. Afterward, grave robbers had stolen the ring, and one of them had stored it in his pocket space. Sadly, because of a falling out between the robbers, the owner of the pocket space lost his life. The ring had sat in there for decades, but Seraphie had finally made her way back to Quartz.

Quartz was on a high that could put the happy newlywed Jade to shame. He used to be the embodiment of possessiveness back when Seraphie was still alive, never letting her out in public. Thankfully, he seemed to have relaxed some, because Seraphie could be seen walking around the castle from time to time.

At first, the people in the castle had panicked and screamed at the ghost in their midst, but once they learned that it was Quartz's mate, everyone had shed tears of joy. Nowadays, no one was surprised to see Seraphie roaming around.

Seraphie enjoyed strolling around the castle since she hadn't been able to do so while alive, but she spent most of her time during the day with Quartz. Knowing that, Ruri wondered if it would be okay for her to go somewhere Quartz couldn't follow, like the pocket space.

"Will Quartz-sama be upset if you go?" Ruri asked.

"He's helping the king with his duties, so he'll be fine," Seraphie replied.

"I don't mind if you come, but shouldn't you say something to him first?"

Since Seraphie was a ghost, she could stay in the pocket space without any issues, but if she were to suddenly leave without explanation, Quartz would probably hassle the outside world in general.

Seraphie, however, smiled cheerfully and said, "It'll be fine. Just fine. I want to move around as I please."

When she'd been alive, Seraphie had remained sheltered from the public out of respect for Quartz's wishes, but now she was enjoying her newfound freedom. It probably gave Quartz a headache, given his stronger-than-usual attachment to her, but it seemed that not even he could restrict Seraphie after she'd been locked in a small pocket space room for decades.

"Well then, I'm ready. Are you?" asked Ruri.

"Yes. We can go at any time," Seraphie replied.

Ruri asked herself if it would really be okay. She was worried that Quartz would yell at her later. Nonetheless, she opened her pocket space and hopped inside with her tea and cookies.

Ruri's pocket space was filled with a multitude of items, as always. She'd inherited many of them from Lydia's previous contract-bearer, the first Dragon King, Weidt. A portrait of him hung on the wall.

Ruri knew that Lydia would tenderly gaze at the portrait. Weidt was very special to Lydia. Even if Ruri wasn't able to fill that hole, she at least wanted to help Lydia enjoy herself in any way possible.

"Oh, Lydia~! I'm here!" Ruri announced.

Lydia phased into view and smiled in delight.

"*Welcome, Ruri. And you too, Seraphie.*"

"Thank you for having me, O Spirit of Time," Seraphie replied, politely bowing to Lydia.

"I made you some cookies," Ruri said.

She placed the cookies and tea on the table Lydia had set and then took a seat. Lydia and Seraphie followed soon after.

"*I haven't had your cookies in so long!*" Lydia said, her eyes lighting up.

Seeing her face, Ruri felt racked with guilt.

"I'm sorry I haven't stopped by as of late."

"*Tee hee hee. It's fine. You are a newlywed now. They say that dragonkin are jealous, so I assume the king wouldn't let you leave his side, yes?*"

"More or less."

"*It's no problem to me if it's no problem to you. But if that dragonkin clinginess becomes too much to bear, just let me know. I'll ensure that you can make a getaway,*" Lydia said with a very cheeky wink.

Ruri smiled awkwardly, replying, "Rin pretty much said the same thing to me. It's appreciated, but are dragonkin really so problematic that you need to warn people about them?"

"Of course they are!" confirmed Seraphie, the senior dragonkin mate. "In the beginning, I was elated that such a handsome man passionately confessed to me, and I found myself falling in love not long after. And, well, that isn't problematic in and of itself, but if I talked to a member of the opposite sex, he would come up and intimidate me with that smile. His harmless looks caught me off guard and, before I knew it, he brought me to the Nation of the Dragon King, married me, and locked me away from people."

Ruri had heard that Quartz's confinement had been... thorough.

"Didn't you resist, Seraphie-san?"

"I did!" Seraphie insisted. "But when he admonished me with that gentle smile, I nodded my head...and let him cajole me into agreeing." She saw the exasperated look on Ruri's face and blurted out, "I mean, how was I supposed to resist?! Quartz's face is *exactly* my type! You would nod and say 'yes' if a face like that asked you for a favor, *right*? *Right*?!"

"Aha ha... U-Um, well, Quartz *is* especially handsome for a dragonkin," Ruri said. She could understand Seraphie's feelings since Jade was a good-looking man himself. If someone with his looks were to appear depressed in front of her, she would present her paw pads to him in a heartbeat.

"I suggest that you be careful, Ruri. If you don't secure your territory while you can, then he'll encroach on you and eventually shut you in. The dragonkin are *extremely* obsessive," Seraphie warned her. Then she added with flushed cheeks, "But, well, their loving nature *is* one of their good traits."

Ruri wanted to ask *which* point she was trying to make.

"Whether you feel loved or whether you feel constricted depends on the individual. How about you, Ruri? Are you okay with it?" Seraphie asked.

"Yes. I don't feel constricted for the time being," Ruri replied. She was glad to see Jade fully expressing his love.

"That's good to hear, then. Still, heed my warning. There is one thing that you *must* adhere to."

"What is it?" Ruri asked, listening intensely.

"Don't *ever* make him jealous. Be careful, especially when talking to the opposite sex. If you so much as try to strike up some friendly conversation, they'll lock you in the bedroom and won't let you out until morning."

"I'll…be careful."

Both Ruri and Lydia suspected that Seraphie had been speaking from personal experience given the awfully specific nature of her words.

The three girls chatted idly as they enjoyed their tea and cookies. Being a ghost, Seraphie wasn't partaking in the refreshments, but she provided the party with plenty to talk about. As a former witch of Yadacain, she talked at length about the country's history, its witches, and their sorcery—all of which Ruri knew nothing about.

"Apparently, the witches of Yadacain stayed in the Nation of the Dragon King at some point. The witches used their own brand of magic that didn't employ the spirits' power, but people called their sorcery 'witchcraft' and feared it, believing that it cursed people. In actuality, cursing people is such an advanced skill that there were hardly any who could do it. Facing persecution for simply being capable of such feats, they left their homeland and drifted over to the Nation of the Dragon King. Relations soured even there, and the witches took to the sea, where they founded the nation we now know as Yadacain. The first queen was quite young, but she was said to possess immense power as a witch. Sadly, she died young due to illness."

"*Oh, but that's not accurate,*" Lydia interjected.

"Huh?" murmured Seraphie.

"*Yadacain's first queen didn't die of illness. She was murdered.*"

"She was?"

"*Yes. I would know since Weidt was friends with her. When he heard she was dead, Weidt flew off in a rage and stormed to Yadacain.*"

"Did he know who killed her?" Ruri questioned, resting her chin in her hand.

"*The next in line to be queen.*"

"Whoa, wasn't that pretty dangerous?" Ruri asked, realizing that the Dragon King storming into a nation like that was likely to kick-start a war.

"*They ended up driving Weidt out. He came to me to grumble and complain about it.*"

"Why would the successor do something like that, though?" Seraphie questioned. She was curious about this new piece of her homeland's history, especially since it differed from what she'd always known.

"*Spirit Slayer started it all. A witch created the Spirit Slayer magic, but the first queen realized its dangers and wouldn't allow them to use it. The witch didn't like that decision and killed the first queen, becoming the queen herself. That's about it.*"

"Oh wow…" Ruri disinterestedly hummed as she stuffed her face with cookies.

"*You may think this doesn't pertain to you, Ruri, but she has a link to you too,*" Lydia stated.

"How so?"

"*The bracelet you use to turn into a cat. The first queen made it and gave it to Weidt. It's been assisting you a great deal thus far, hasn't it?*"

"Yeah, it has, actually," Ruri replied. She couldn't count the number of times that the magic bracelet had helped her out or how many cuddle-starved dragonkin it had comforted.

Seraphie commented, "That cat-transforming bracelet of yours is truly something amazing, Ruri. I don't remember or know *anyone* who has been able to create a magic tool that can transform one so perfectly."

A magic tool was an item that contained the magical power of mana. Seraphie explained that there were two types of magic tools: ones that utilized the user's own mana to activate and ones that used a solidified stone of mana called a magic stone.

"And it's even *more* difficult to make something with a semipermanent effect like your bracelet."

The raiders who attacked Ruri before had carried a bracelet that turned people into rats, but it had a limited number of uses. Humans without mana could use it, but it would become useless once the mana in the magic stone was consumed. Seraphie admitted that she could, in theory, create one herself.

There were supposedly only a handful who could make a bracelet with unlimited usage like Ruri's. Ruri's bracelet would activate as long as the user had mana. If someone without mana were to wear it, it would be just a normal bracelet. But as long as they had mana to power it, the bracelet could be used forever. Because of that, it was difficult to make, and Seraphie's attempts to explain the process sounded like gibberish to Ruri.

"Would it be hard for even *you* to craft one, Seraphie-san?" Ruri asked.

Seraphie was a skilled witch, powerful enough to seal her own soul into a ring.

Be that as it may, Seraphie replied, "Hmm. That might be a little much for me. I think I could *only just* make one if I copied yours."

"Wouldn't it explode in popularity if you sold it?"

In this world—especially in the Nation of the Dragon King where humans and demi-humans coexisted without discrimination—there were plenty of humans who wished to change into animals, and demi-humans who wanted to turn into other races. Ruri would sometimes overhear the dragonkin who worked at the castle wishing they could be cats or admiring fluffier demi-humans.

Ruri and Seraphie looked at each other and grinned deviously.

"We might be able to make a *ton* of money," Seraphie concluded.

Ruri thought for a moment and said, "Should we sell them to the dragonkin first?"

That was when Seraphie realized there was a problem.

"Aah, we can't, though."

"Why can't we?" asked Ruri.

"We don't have any magic stones. If it were a simple magic tool, then you wouldn't need a stone to act as a conduit for the magic. But when it comes to advanced magic like shapeshifting, I won't be able to do it myself unless I use magic stones."

"You can make simple ones without them?"

"Yes. I mean, if I had the power and wisdom of the first queen, who made your bracelet, I might be able to create bracelets without magic stones, but I certainly can't do it on my own. I collected some in Yadacain, but you won't find many just lying around…"

Seraphie let her eyes wander around the room until she spotted something and gasped.

"Oh!"

Ruri followed her gaze to a mountain of gemstones on the floor. She didn't know what kind of gemstones they were, but there were plenty of them littering the room. She'd inherited them from Weidt. They were so clear, sparkly, and beautiful that she'd gathered them all in one place. The resulting pile was well over Ruri's height.

"*Those are magic stones,*" Lydia stated.

"Huh?! Are you serious?!"

"Yes. I guess they really were just lying around. How convenient."

According to Seraphie, magic stones took years to form, and only in places with a large concentration of natural mana. Finding those places was by no means an easy task.

Lydia knew the reason Weidt had owned so many, so she explained, "*Magic stones used to be so abundant in Yadacain that you could find them strewn all over. Weidt used to pick them up and collect them. However, the Spirit Slayer absorbed the mana in the earth, causing their numbers to dwindle. Now that Spirit Slayer has been wiped from Yadacain, I imagine that magic stones will gradually start to multiply.*"

"Spirit Slayer really doesn't do any good, does it?" Ruri commented.

"When you put it that way, I feel somewhat guilty," Seraphie replied. She was from Yadacain and had benefited from Spirit Slayer up until Quartz took her away. She probably felt conflicted in more ways than one, but she perked up and said, "Still, I can create as many bracelets as I please with these!"

"Lydia, can we use them?" Yuri asked.

"*I don't mind. Everything you see here belongs to you, Ruri. Use anything as you see fit. Magic stones are nothing more than junk to people who don't know how to use them, anyway.*"

Weidt had enjoyed collecting all of the stones, but he'd left them in storage since he hadn't known how to use them.

"In that case, I'll help myself," Ruri said.

"Tee hee hee. With this many stones, we can easily become billionaires," Seraphie declared. She couldn't stop smiling.

Her mind filled with the prospect of rolling in oodles and oodles of cash, Ruri exclaimed, "Yes, and I'll help too!"

"*Ruri, shouldn't you be keeping by the king's side instead of doing that? You haven't finished tuning the dragonheart yet, right?*" Lydia prodded.

Ruri's cheeks instantly heated up. "H-H-H-How do *you* know that?!" she asked, panicking.

34

Lydia cocked her head, her expression blank. *"Did I say something to disturb you? I know looks can deceive, but I am a spirit. I can find out something as simple as that without asking. After all, I can sense a different mana inside of you."*

"O-Oh, really?"

"The sooner you tune up, the better. The human body is weak. You'll be tougher once you're tuned, which will be a relief for me too."

Lydia had said that as if it were nothing, but in order to tune the dragonheart, Ruri had to kiss Jade. The very thought of it turned Ruri's cheeks positively red.

"Oh my, you're not ready yet, Ruri?" asked Seraphie, the experienced spouse among them. "Well, I guess that makes sense seeing as it takes time with humans. It took quite a while for me too. But even though it did strengthen my body, I died of illness," she said with a cheerful chuckle. There wasn't an iota of doom or gloom in her voice; she was an extremely bright and cheery ghost.

Since Seraphie was more experienced, Ruri asked her, "Um, so, Seraphie-san… When you were tuning, did you also, well, you know…"

"Are you asking if I kissed?" Seraphie said without hesitation.

"Um, yes…"

Seraphie nodded. "It was a shock to me too when I first heard it. I never would've thought that kissing was necessary for the synchronization process."

"Personally, I don't know if I'll be able to handle it…" Ruri said. The whole process made her want to die of embarrassment.

"You just have to bear with it," Seraphie said with a look of calm resignation that Ruri couldn't help but admire. "There's no other way, from what I've been told. I was embarrassed half to death too, but I stuck with it. That is the fate of dragonkin spouses."

Ruri was already making a lot of concessions, so to speak. "Just *who* does kissing to tune this thing really benefit?!" she retorted.

35

"Aha ha ha… Well, it did put Quartz in a good mood. Still, you'll just have to concede on this."

"Unghh…"

As Ruri and Seraphie talked at length about the synchronization process, Lydia timidly interjected, *"Erm… You don't need to kiss to tune a dragonheart."*

"Huh…?!"

"Huh?!"

Both Ruri and Seraphie loudly gasped and turned toward Lydia.

"You tune a dragonheart by simply transferring mana to the person. All you need to do is touch any spot on their body."

"Huh? Does that mean…?" Ruri started.

"Simply holding hands would suffice," Lydia confirmed.

"Say *what*?!" Ruri exclaimed.

"Excuse me?!" Seraphie hollered.

They were both stunned.

"But Jade-sama said it was necessary!"

"And Quartz said that as well!"

"M-Maybe the two of you were tricked, then?"

A single emotion started to bubble up from deep inside both women—anger.

"Seraphie-san!"

"Right behind you, Ruri!"

The two looked at one another, opened up an exit from the pocket space, and started walking toward it.

"Lydia, I'll see you later. Some *minor business* just popped up," Ruri called over her shoulder.

Seraphie added, "Thank you for having us, O Spirit of Time."

"Oh dear," Lydia said to herself with a wry smile as she watched them leave her behind.

Ruri ran as fast as she could, Seraphie right by her side, from the pocket space to the royal office. She knocked on the door with enough force to break it down before she entered. There she found Jade, looking back at her with wide eyes. As luck would have it, Quartz was also there.

"What's wrong, Ruri? You look angry for some reason," Jade questioned.

Ruri stood in front of Jade, flashed him a scary smile, and asked, "Jade-sama, you can tune a dragonheart by just holding hands, *can't you*?!"

Seraphie then pressed Quartz, saying, "The Spirit of Time told us. You said that kissing was necessary for the tuning, didn't you? So that means you *tricked* me?!"

Jade and Quartz remained silent for a second before they averted their eyes and clicked their tongues.

"Tch, the secret's out," Jade murmured.

"She should have minded her own business," Quartz whispered.

Despite their mumbling, Ruri and Seraphie heard them loud and clear.

"Jade-samaaaa!"

"Quarrrrtz!"

The two ladies were seething, and the men were beginning to panic.

"No, wait, Ruri. I was just, you see... Um, well..."

"Calm down, Seraphie. I did it out of love."

As the two of them tried to worm their way out of this situation, Ruri and Seraphie turned their backs to them.

"R-Ruri?"

"Seraphie?"

They reached out, only to grab nothing but air.

"Jade-sama, I'm imposing a *cuddle ban* for the time being!" Ruri declared.

Jade's jaw almost fell off his face. "No, please hold on. Anything but that…"

Cuddling cured what ailed Jade the most, and there was no greater form of penance he could endure than having that taken away from him.

Ruri, however, barked, "No! I won't turn into a cat in front of you anymore because of your lies, Jade-sama!"

"And as for you, Quartz, I'm not going to show myself to you for a while," Seraphie asserted.

Quartz was also panicking. "What are you saying, Seraphie?!" he cried.

"I'm saying that this is the most effective punishment for you."

"Wait. Hold on, please!" Quartz screamed, running toward Seraphie, but Seraphie turned transparent until she eventually melted into thin air.

She'd most likely gone back inside the ring that housed her soul. Quartz had the ring in his possession, but there was nothing he could do now that Seraphie had retreated.

"Seraphie! Seraphie!" Quartz desperately yelled at the ring. Deafening silence was the only response he got.

"Jade-sama, Quartz-sama, you two need to think about what you've done!" Ruri yelled as a parting remark before exiting the office.

The Path to Forgiveness

Because of his lie about mana tuning, Jade was under a cuddle ban. He had tried to plead with Ruri for forgiveness, looking sad and sympathetic, but his attempt was met with silence. Dark clouds had gathered between them in the midst of their lovey-dovey newlywed period.

"Ruri…" Jade murmured.

Ruri would normally lay in cat form on Jade's lap, but she was currently sitting far away from him, enjoying a friendly cup of tea with Kotaro, Rin, and the other spirits—as if she were taunting him. Jade's sorrowful cry was promptly ignored.

Meanwhile, Quartz would talk to the ring whenever he had a free moment, but the occupant was still too angry to reply to him. Seraphie had been a dragonkin mate for much longer than Ruri, so she probably felt even *more* betrayed. Ruri wasn't going to step in and mediate either, considering she was also upset she'd been fed the same exact lie.

Ruri was stunned that Jade had taken advantage of her ignorance to make her believe his self-serving lies. She had trusted him from the bottom of her heart, and the rage she felt was immense.

Several days had passed, and Jade had reached his limit. His cuddle deficiency was flaring up.

"Ruri, I can't take it anymore! I need my fix!"

"Oh, I see. And?" Ruri replied in an icy tone, not even giving him a passing look.

Jade dropped to his knees and took Ruri's hand. "It was all my fault. I just knew that you were bashful, so I gave in to an urge against my better judgment—that if I told you that, you would accept it. I swear to you that I will never tell such a lie ever again. So, please… Please, turn into a cat for me!"

Ruri was stunned that Jade was so starved for something soft in just a few days' time. He was pleading his case with such sincere passion in his eyes that it was quite the pathetic sight. Jade's appearance was of the highest caliber, yet despite his good looks, he was a somewhat unfortunate man. *This* was the ruler of the Nation of the Dragon King. If any of his subjects were to see him in this state, they might be a tad apprehensive about the nation's future. That said, Jade did appear to be wholeheartedly sorry for his actions, so Ruri decided it was time to bury the hatchet.

Ruri heaved a sigh before facing Jade and saying, "If you *ever* tell me a stupid lie like that again, I'm divorcing you on the spot."

"Huh? Divorce?" Jade repeated as his face muscles twitched.

"Any problems with that?" Ruri asked, shooting a glare at him.

Jade shook his head furiously. "None! Absolutely none!"

"Also, no kissing until the tuning is done."

"No *what*?!"

"This is your punishment for lying to me, Jade-sama."

"But you already had me on a *cuddle ban*, didn't you?!"

"That is one thing, and this is another. It's fine, right, since we can tune my mana without kissing?"

"N-No, but, you see…" Jade stammered, his eyes darting all around.

Ruri smiled sweetly and cooed, "You'll show me that you can be sincere, right?"

"Right…" Jade agreed. He slumped and mumbled under his breath, "Even though we're *newlyweds*…"

Ruri heard his hushed comment, but she ignored it. Looking at her completely disheartened husband, she pulled out her bracelet and put it on, turning into a cat for the first time in a while.

Jade started quivering in excitement.

"You can hold me."

"Grk. My first cuddle in forever!"

Although she was exasperated at Jade, who was on the verge of tears, Ruri walked up to him. He timidly reached out to her, scooping her soft and fluffy body up into his arms.

"I was in total *agony* not being able to touch you, Ruri…"

"Then let this serve as a lesson to never deceive me again."

"If this is what I have to go through, then I *never* will again."

Ruri secretly considered using this punishment again in the future should the need arise.

While Ruri and Jade's reconciliation transpired, things on Seraphie and Quartz's end were also progressing. Feeling pity for Quartz, who was starting to look haggard from the stress, the Spirit of Light intervened, convincing Seraphie to reluctantly leave the ring. Seraphie still gave him a very stern lecture after she reappeared, but Quartz was so overjoyed to see her that it was doubtful whether he actually heard a word she said.

Now that Ruri had forgiven him, Jade sat with her in cat form on his lap, looking over paperwork.

Ruri and Seraphie's punishment had unexpectedly affected more than just the Dragon King and his predecessor. The mental drain of being apart from their loved ones had reduced the nation's dynamic duo into useless messes, hampering their work. Thanks to this, Jade's desk was piled high with paperwork.

Claus had scolded Ruri and pleaded with her to report to him in advance the next time she did something like that. Ruri had no idea that Jade would get so down that it would impede his kingly duties, so she sincerely apologized—not to Jade, of course, but to Claus and the other aides whom she'd inconvenienced as a result.

The situation had been the most stressful for the chancellor of the kingdom, Euclase. They were still griping about the whole ordeal even now, right in front of her.

"I swear. Being newlyweds is fine. Having fights is also fine. However, I would much appreciate it if you didn't bring that trouble our way. Thanks to your antics, I haven't been getting *nearly* enough sleep, and it's been *chapping my skin.*"

"*I apologize,*" Ruri replied, bending to Euclase's pressure. "*Y-You still look beautiful, Euclase-san.*"

Ruri was trying to flatter Euclase a bit in order to raise their mood, but Euclase glared at her for some reason and said, "Well, *of course* I am. Just how much money and effort do you think I put into my beauty regimen? In fact, you ought to pay closer attention to your *own* cosmetics. Youth alone will only carry you so far!"

"*R-Right!*" Ruri answered, her feline tail standing straight on end.

"Also, you aren't even in tune, are you? Why aren't you done yet? You've been together for so long."

That was actually Jade's fault. He'd only been giving her mana when they kissed, though holding hands would have sufficed. That was why it was taking so long. It was all Jade's fault for lying—not Ruri's at all.

Now, thanks to the kissing ban she'd imposed until the tuning was finished, Jade had been actively touching Ruri's head and hands to circulate mana into her body. If he had simply done that from the beginning, then the process would have been finished long ago.

It was entirely fair to say that Jade was to blame. Jade seemed to know that himself, because he awkwardly turned away from Ruri and Euclase.

"After you're tuned up," Euclase explained, "you'll age as slowly as a dragonkin, so the sooner the better."

"Oh wow, is that so?"

Ruri still couldn't imagine aging as gracefully as dragonkin, who didn't reach adulthood until they turned one hundred.

"Well, either way, Ruri would have lived a long time because of her mana," Jade said while patting Ruri's head.

In this world, the amount of mana you had affected your life span. Even among humans, there was a difference in how they aged after reaching adulthood depending on whether they had mana. Riccia, Ruri's mother, and Beryl, Ruri's grandfather, appeared young for their ages due to their mana.

Ruri had known for a while now that dragonkin had a long life span, so she was relieved to learn that she would be able to match Jade's. It meant that she would have that much more time to be with him. On the other hand, that would also affect the amount of time she would have to live without her parents and grandfather. She decided not to think too deeply about it for the time being.

Now that Euclase's sermon was over, more work piled up on Jade's desk, making Jade grimace. Nevertheless, he needed to reap what he sowed. Ruri tried to be invisible and stay out of the way, but suddenly, and without warning, the door flung open. Euclase and Claus raised their eyebrows, wondering who would enter the Dragon King's office without knocking, but their expressions quickly relaxed once they saw who it was. It was an individual who had no relation to the human world's rules—the Spirit of Light.

Not daring to call the supreme-level Spirit of Light impudent, Euclase moved to the side and opened a path straight to Jade.

"What can I help you with?" Jade asked politely.

"I'm not here for you. That's what I'm here for," the Spirit of Light said, pointing to Ruri. As soon as Ruri cocked her head in confusion, the Spirit of light grabbed her by the scruff of her neck. "Seraphie wants to see her. I'm going to take her there."

Before Jade could even agree to it, the Spirit of Light left the room with what she'd come for.

The Spirit of Light, a supreme-level spirit in a form so adorable that she could be mistaken for a bisque doll, held Ruri by the neck still as Ruri dangled in the air. There were probably dragonkin who would secretly writhe at the sight of these two in the castle.

"*What is it that she needs?*" Ruri asked.

"No clue. You'll have to ask her. She's apparently been busy making something lately."

"*Ah, maybe it's* that," Ruri guessed.

The Spirit of Light brought Ruri to Quartz's quarters. Quartz was out because of work, but Seraphie was in.

"*Seraphie-san?*"

After the Spirit of Light lowered her to the ground, Ruri trotted over to Seraphie. She saw several bracelets scattered around. They looked very similar to the one she was currently wearing, confirming that her hunch had been correct.

"Tee hee hee hee. I've done it, Ruri. They're done!"

"*You really did it?!*"

"Yes. This one is a rabbit. This is a squirrel. This is a dog. And I've made a bunch more too!"

Seraphie showed her bracelets to Ruri with a look of satisfaction and pride. They were all replicas of Ruri's cat-transformation bracelet.

Although they were of lesser quality and capability than the one made by the first queen of Yadacain, these magic tools were the best that Seraphie could come up with.

In order to make these, Ruri and Seraphie had asked the dragonkin castle workers what animal they'd like to turn into. Their answers culminated in the several bracelets that lay before them.

"*How many times can you use these?*" Ruri asked.

"Only about three times a piece for now. But with a little more research, I think I can increase the number of uses."

"*Oooh. You're the best, Seraphie-san!*"

"Tee hee hee, keep the praise coming," Seraphie said with her head held high. "Still, we need to test them before we start selling them."

"*Then let's go out and look for people to be our test subjects right now!*"

Since there were always dragonkin training there, Ruri and Seraphie went to the training grounds in Sector Five.

Ever since the conflict with Yadacain had ended, things had been extremely peaceful—meaning that the dragonkin soldiers were bored and without a battle outlet. Ruri had no problem with things being peaceful, but the combat-crazed dragonkin were finding it unsatisfactory. They put all their frustrations into their training, so the grounds were much more intense than usual.

Ruri, however, was here to deliver some comfort to the ailing soldiers. "Attention, everyone!" she yelled after she'd returned to human form.

The training dragonkin stopped what they were doing. Ruri had gotten pretty used to the blood-drenched soldiers' appearances. Some of them even stood there with all sorts of weapons sticking out of their body. It would be a personal loss if she were to keep letting it bother her.

The soldiers approached Ruri, curious to see what was going on.

"Whatever is the matter, Lady Beloved?" asked a soldier.

"Okay, everyone," Ruri called. "Do you remember the survey I took a while back?"

"Yes. When you asked us those weird questions about what animals we'd like to turn into."

"What did you answer?" Ruri asked the crowd.

"I picked a cat," replied one soldier.

"I picked a sheep," replied another.

"Heh heh heh, I picked…" started another soldier until all of them were rambling about the animals they wanted to be.

Ruri pulled out a bracelet and asked, "By the way, who said they wanted to be a rabbit?"

Several of the soldiers raised their hands.

"Okay, those of you who want to *actually* be a rabbit!" Ruri asked again, double-checking.

The men with their hands raised shot puzzled looks at one another, but then an astute soldier looked at the bracelet Ruri was holding and stepped forward faster than anyone else.

"Here, here! Heeere! Me, please!"

"A great response! Well then, please put on that bracelet," Ruri instructed.

Most of the soldiers could more or less piece together what was going on.

"Huh? No way. Seriously?"

"Is this for real?"

"That can really turn you into one?"

As questions flew left and right, all eyes were on the soldier holding the bracelet. They all watched with bated breath as he put it on. In the next instant, he transformed into a rabbit.

The crowd cheered loudly.

"Whoaaaa!"

"A rabbit! It's a rabbit!"

"Hey, let me touch you!"

"Oooh, so soft and fluffy!"

"Pass it to me!"

The soldier that had turned into a rabbit was getting mobbed. He squirmed in panic, but everyone was too excited to notice the rabbit's cries for help.

Sensing that the rabbit would be crushed to death at this rate, Ruri shouted, "Okay, stoooop! Calm down! Anyone who doesn't move away from that rabbit right now won't be allowed to touch me ever again when I turn into a cat!" Granted, Ruri never expected that Jade would allow any other man to touch her now that she was officially his mate, but it was a conditioned reflex.

The crowd cleared away from the rabbit like a receding wave. The rescued rabbit took off the bracelet, and the soldier turned back into his original form.

"I-I thought I was a goner..." the soldier gasped.

Ruri couldn't blame him for thinking that, considering how a bunch of huge, hulking men had ganged up on him. It was likely that the soldiers had considered the rabbit a strong and sturdy dragonkin, unlike the weak and frail Ruri in cat form, so none of them had held back. He'd almost ended up torn to shreds. Ruri realized that perhaps she had *slightly* underestimated the dragonkin's love for soft and cuddly animals.

"By the way, this one has a limited number of uses, unlike mine. So give us your honest feedback. Would you want this if I sold it?"

As soon as she asked, the soldiers rushed over, crying, "Yes! Yes!"

"I'd want one!"

"I'll pay any amount!"

Ruri looked at Seraphie and they both grinned.

They needed to test it to see if it would activate correctly, so they picked a number of soldiers to be their testers by drawing lots. The losers broke down in tears on the spot, but they recovered once they heard that they could eventually buy the bracelets. The winners kept their prize. Some said they would use it on their wife, and others said they would use it themselves. They all looked more delighted than Ruri had envisioned. This was the moment she knew that these bracelets would sell.

Unfortunately, there was a big issue. This story reached Euclase, who promptly scolded both Ruri and Seraphie.

"Ruri! Have you forgotten that you were assaulted by Raiders who infiltrated the castle using those to turn into animals?! What will you do if you let those spread out into the wild and they're used for criminal activities?!"

Ruri, who hadn't given the idea that much consideration, lowered her head. "You're absolutely right…"

She'd only thought that other people would enjoy it if they could transform. She turned into a cat on a regular basis without giving the process much thought, so she'd completely forgotten about the possibility of it being used for nefarious purposes. One could say she had also been blinded by the prospect of monetary gain.

Euclase, infuriated at both of them, confiscated all the bracelets and banned them from making any more, which left Ruri and Seraphie feeling blue afterward.

4 Farewell Letter

"I thought I'd be rolling in dough," Ruri lamented. She still couldn't cope with the fact that her bracelets had been banned.

Claus smiled wryly. "Those are just far too dangerous. Euclase wasn't wrong for banning them. I'm grateful that Euclase was able to squash that idea before it went public."

"No, I get it. But still, I can't help thinking how much of a shame it is."

"What's done is done. Just keep them for your own amusement," Jade suggested.

"Yes, sir…" Ruri replied. "So, what was it that you wanted to discuss?"

Jade had told Ruri that he wanted to talk to her, but his tone had sounded strangely formal. Hence, she wasn't sitting in her usual position on Jade's lap, but rather across from him on the couch inside the royal office. Jade seemed unhappy that she wasn't sitting next to him, but a discussion would be easier face-to-face, so she'd made him concede.

"The top brass of the four nations are going to hold a meeting in the Nation of the Spirit King," Jade declared.

"A meeting?" asked Ruri.

"It's nothing major, just a routine gathering to strengthen relations between the four nations. It's always held in the Nation of the Spirit King because it's historically the oldest among the four and because it's where the supreme-level Spirit of Trees resides."

"Oh, wow."

"So, yes, I'd like you to come with me."

"Wha? I couldn't do anything even if I did go, though. Any complicated political jargon would go way over my head."

While Ruri was the Dragon King's queen, she was also a Beloved, meaning that she led a life completely divorced from politics. At first, she'd tried to study what a queen should be doing, but she'd been told not to get involved and kept at a distance because a Beloved engaging in political matters would bring about confusion. Ruri was grateful, considering that she'd had no interest in politics in her *home* world, much less *this* world, but there were times when she wondered if that was the right call.

Whenever that thought crossed her mind, Seraphie would come out and say, "I was always a shut-in."

Although Seraphie had remained a shut-in because of Quartz's possessive desire to keep her from the eyes of other men, her advice as the senior dragonkin spouse did convince Ruri that abstaining was the right call. As a result, Ruri stayed out of the nation's affairs unless necessary.

Since that was the easiest way to deal with being both a queen and a Beloved, Ruri kept her studies to the bare minimum of common knowledge so that she wouldn't learn anything she wasn't supposed to. In retrospect, offering aid to the slums by introducing a school lunch system was toeing the line. Then again, given that she'd only suggested the idea and Euclase had done all the work, it was probably *just* barely passable.

"You don't need to talk about politics," Jade assured her. "Leave that to the other kings and me. But I thought you should participate from now on since there are always other Beloveds attending."

Jade mentioned the other Beloveds as an incentive for Ruri to go, even though the pact between the four major nations stated that it was *not* recommended that Beloveds of different nations meet. It could result in unnecessary damage if the Beloveds were to disagree.

For example, the fight between Ruri and the Beloved of Cerulanda had been completely unexpected. Nothing disastrous had happened because not only was Ruri's status as a Beloved higher, but she also had a supreme-level spirit like Kotaro by her side. On the other hand, if the opposing Beloved had been higher in rank than Ruri, the spirits would have promptly turned on her. The pact was instituted to prevent those sorts of incidents.

Beloveds bestowed blessings, but they also bestowed chaos. Gathering that many Beloveds under one roof would make matters even worse. However, in the case of Beloveds from the four great nations, the Spirit of Trees in the Nation of the Spirit King acted as a mediator in case of disputes, so it was never an issue for Beloveds to attend the meeting.

Ruri thought the Spirit of Trees should do the same for other Beloveds as well, but it was said that the supreme-level spirit would not act for any nation unaffiliated with its own and not part of the union. The Spirit of Trees would only intervene when it benefited the Nation of the Spirit King. Their reasons for doing so were unknown, but just as Kotaro and Rin would never act on anyone's behalf other than Ruri's or the spirits', the Spirit of Trees wouldn't act without a similar reason of their own. And that reason was none of Ruri's business.

Ruri asked, "The other Beloveds would be Celestine and Lapis, right?"

"Yes. The Imperial Nation doesn't have a Beloved," answered Jade.

Ruri was already acquainted with both Celestine and Lapis. Celestine still hadn't completely given up her feelings for Jade, and Lapis was morbidly in love with Ruri. Both Beloveds had their issues, but Ruri knew they weren't bad people, which made her feel better.

"You should speak with them while we're having our meeting," Jade suggested. "But be careful of Lapis. Don't let him lay even a finger on you."

"I don't think I have to be *that* wary. He most likely has already found someone new."

Jade still seemed concerned about how Lapis had told Ruri that he was smitten with her, but it wouldn't be surprising if the lovesick boy had fallen in love at first sight with someone different the next day. In fact, Ruri was probably out of his mind by now.

"No, you need to be *extremely* cautious. He is dangerous," Jade warned, furrowing his brow.

Claus, who was looking on, simply shrugged in resignation. This was probably business as usual for male dragonkin.

"Okay, then I'll just spend my time chatting with Celestine-san," Ruri conceded.

"Yes, please do."

Just as Ruri thought that their discussion was finished, Claus's expression turned stern and he asked, "Your Majesty, shouldn't you talk to Ruri about *you-know-what* as well?"

"No, but…" Jade stammered.

"Ruri is a central player in this issue. There should be several nobles in the Imperial Nation's entourage coming to the meeting, so it's in Ruri's best interest to know beforehand instead of after the fact. I know it's not a very pleasant topic, but…"

"Yes, it isn't," Jade agreed.

Ruri tilted her head and asked, "What is it? What are you both talking about?"

Jade's expression also turned stern as he replied, "It could be a rather unpleasant subject. Are you sure?"

"It pertains to me, doesn't it? I'll listen."

Jade hesitated, then said, "You see, several of the Imperial Nation's nobles are launching complaints at the Nation of the Dragon King."

"Complaints?" Ruri repeated. Nothing worth complaining about came to mind.

"Currently, the Nation of the Dragon King has three Beloveds: you, your mother, and your grandfather. The Imperial Nation, on the other hand, doesn't have a single Beloved to their name. Thus, the nobles are voicing their apprehensions about us housing three Beloveds, citing that it upsets the balance of the four nations."

"But neither my mother, my grandpa, nor I have done anything," Ruri protested.

"Just a Beloved's presence has a massive impact on all around them," Jade explained. "Spirits are plentiful, and soil becomes fertile wherever a Beloved stays. That is especially true with three of them in one place."

"Ah, I see." Ruri remembered that she'd felt like there were more spirits around the castle lately. She hadn't paid it any mind, but it was probably because two more Beloveds were now in the kingdom.

"They're worried that the Nation of the Dragon King will gain more influence at this rate," Jade continued. "I mean, it's just a bunch of power-hungry nobles howling in jealousy, but there seems to be more of a vocal majority in the Imperial Nation than I thought. My guess is that they're paranoid because the other three nations have Beloveds, while they don't have even one. According to the emperor of the Imperial Nation, Adularia, some foolish nobles are suggesting that they *buy* one of our nation's Beloveds from us."

"'Buy us'? We're not *things*," Ruri huffed.

"Indeed, but there are a surprising number of fools who are seriously considering that as an option, giving Adularia nothing but headaches."

Ruri had met Emperor Adularia at the wedding. She was a gorgeous woman who emanated sophistication with a sort of East Asian flair. She looked young, but Ruri had been shocked to learn that she was actually a mother of four children around Ruri's age. In terms of mothers who looked young for their age, she was on par with the mana-rich Riccia. Admittedly, back in their home world, people had often thought that Riccia was Ruri's sister.

"What should we do, then?" Ruri asked.

"The best option would be to do as the nobles say and let one of our Beloveds go to the Imperial Nation," Jade answered. "But we can't force a Beloved to do that. Also, I'm not keen on separating your family now that you've finally reunited."

Nodding his head, Claus interjected, "But I'm certain that the nobles of the Imperial Nation will not stay quiet. They might try to contact Ruri during the meeting."

"How should I deal with them?" questioned Ruri. She looked up at Claus standing by Jade's side, knowing that she wouldn't do well if approached about complicated political matters.

"You needn't do anything. You can just smile and ignore them. Where a Beloved goes is a Beloved's choice. No one can twist their arm into doing anything. What's more, you cannot go to the Imperial Nation since you are already the Dragon Queen."

"But what if they try to directly negotiate with my mom or grandpa?"

"We will not be taking either of them to this meeting, so the nobles will never get the chance," Claus answered.

"Well, I feel like my mom will whine about wanting to go, but…"

Riccia had been oddly quiet as of late, but she was normally an active person, so she was likely to be the first in line if she heard about the prospect of a trip.

"We have no choice but to convince them to abstain," Claus stated. "Personally speaking, we find the claims of the Imperial Nation's nobles to be slightly hard to stomach."

Jade nodded in agreement. "No offense to Adularia, but I have no intention of meeting these nobles' demands. Ruri, please keep this secret from your parents and Lord Beryl. I don't want to worry them unnecessarily. We'll handle this issue."

"Very well," Ruri replied, nodding.

The discussion was soon brought to a close, but neither Jade nor Claus realized that someone was listening in from outside the room.

Listening outside the office door was Ruri's grandfather, Beryl.

"Hmm, looks like our arrival is causing problems for Ruri's husband," Beryl groaned, his arms folded.

Another man stood beside him, also listening in. It was Beryl's travel partner for the first half of his stay in this world, the former Beast King and Claus's father, Andal. He patted Beryl on the shoulder and said, "A lot of the Imperial Nation's nobles are a greedy bunch who only have their own interests in mind. This is pretty much expected behavior. Don't tear yourself up over it."

"Still, it kind of bothers me to pretend I don't know that my presence is inconveniencing Ruri."

Even after they'd walked away from the royal office, Beryl continued to hem and haw to himself.

Trotting by Beryl's side near his feet was the supreme-level Spirit of Earth, Chi. At first, Chi had made a contract with Ruri, but as soon as he got to know Beryl's personality, he'd quickly canceled his contract with Ruri and made a new one with Beryl. Since Chi lived on momentum and whim, he seemed to mesh well with Beryl. Likewise, he also seemed to get along with Beryl's travel companion, Andal.

"*Man, humans sure can be a hassle and a half,*" Chi quipped. From his perspective as a spirit, humans were far too strict and rigid.

"That's humans in a nutshell," Beryl replied.

"*Uh-huh...*" Chi trailed off, thinking that things were much more simple and clean in his mind—something was either fun or it wasn't.

Just then, a brilliant idea hit Chi. "*Hey, hey, listen.*"

"What's up?" Beryl asked.

"*The main issue is that there are three Beloveds in the Nation of the Dragon King, right?*"

"Yeah, that's about the gist of it."

"*In that case, all you gotta do is leave the kingdom.*"

As if he were struck by lightning, Beryl gasped and shouted, "Eureka! You're right!"

"*Ain't I, though? I sure am smart~!*" Chi said triumphantly with his head held high.

Beryl reached down and patted him on the head. "I originally came here in search of new land, after all. Plus, I've already been to Ruri's wedding, so there's really no need for me to stay here."

"*Yup, yup.*"

"Hey, hold on, now..." Andal said with an awkward smile as he watched Beryl and Chi jovially nod their heads at one another.

"There's no time like the present! I've made up my mind, so it's time to act today!"

"And I'm coming too~!"

This was just the kind of behavior expected from the freewheeling Chi and the contract-bearer who approved of him.

"What about you, Andal?" asked Beryl.

As his friend and the spirit were staring at him with hopeful eyes, Andal couldn't possibly refuse. "Well, I was planning on leaving soon, so I *could* go."

"Then it's settled!" Beryl exclaimed, giving a thumbs up with a nice, toothy grin.

The next morning, a maid went to Beryl's room, only to find it completely emptied. She rushed out and went to make a report.

The only thing left in the room was a single scrap of paper— a letter that read:

"I heard that too many Beloveds are causing you issues, so I took Chi and Andal out to go on an adventure. I'll come back every once in a while, so don't you worry. I want to see the entire world with my own two eyes! An adventure... That sure does have a nice ring to it."

After Ruri finished reading the brief letter, she clutched her head and groaned.

"Grandpaaaa..."

Maybe he would be fine since Chi, a supreme-level spirit, was with him? No, that seemed like a recipe for *even more* disaster. Still, she felt a tiny bit relieved that he was going with Andal, someone knowledgeable in the ways of this world.

Jade was also at a loss for words.

"I'm sorry that my grandpa is far too active for his own good," Ruri apologized.

"Well, I'm sure he'll be okay since he's with Andal," Jade assured her.

"I'm sure we can locate him if I ask Kotaro, but should I?"

"If Lord Beryl himself left because he wished to do so, then we can't restrict a Beloved's actions. And, well…I do share some of the blame for making him worry."

"No, I'm ninety percent sure he used that as an excuse because he wanted to travel," she grumbled, knowing her grandfather all too well. "Should I just do a little check anyway?"

"Yes. With all due respect to Lord Beryl, the fact that our Beloved left the Nation of the Dragon King can be blamed on the Imperial Nation's nobles."

Jade's point was that it was the nobles' statements that had prompted their Beloved to leave. What if something dangerous happened to him on their journey? Would *they* take responsibility if something happened to the Beloved? Jade had half a mind to ask them. But, at the same time, Beryl would be bestowing the blessings of the spirits to other nations as well by traveling around the world. It was also safe to assume that he might even wind up in the Imperial Nation if he wanted. That all depended on Beryl's mood, though.

"Be that as it may, he at least could have said goodbye to me in person," Ruri spat, frustrated that the only farewell she received was a single scrap of paper. Nevertheless, she knew that was typical of her grandfather. "Kotaro, would you mind telling the spirits with my grandpa to inform you as soon as anything happens to him?"

"*Yes, you've got it. I'll have them report periodically.*"

"Thank you." She petted Kotaro on the head, and he energetically wagged his tail in response. "Honestly, this is *totally* something grandpa would do."

Ruri looked up, feeling slightly melancholic. She took solace in the fact that Beryl was out there somewhere underneath the canopy of the great blue sky.

Riccia and Heat

The news that Beryl had left with Chi and Andal soon spread throughout the castle. Oddly enough, the dragonkin soldiers who sparred with Beryl were the most disappointed by his departure.

In contrast, when the news reached Riccia, his daughter, she simply said, "Oh dear." She seemed neither distraught nor sad about the turn of events. Perhaps she'd already had a hunch that this would happen, knowing that Beryl would never stay quietly in one place for very long.

Kotaro and the other spirits didn't seem to feel any particular way about Chi leaving either. The fact that so many supreme-level spirits were gathered in one place was a rarity in itself. Aside from Chi, who represented earth, the castle was home to the Spirits of Wind, Water, Fire, and Light. If you added Lydia to that mix, then that would make six spirits—half of the twelve supreme-level spirits.

Ruri could somewhat understand why the nobles of the Imperial Nation would say that the power balance between the four nations was in jeopardy. This many supreme-level spirits assembled here made the kingdom much more powerful, not to mention the Beloveds the nation housed. Then again, aside from Kotaro and Rin, the two spirits under Ruri's subjugation, the others stayed of their own free will. But their presence alone was probably enough to instill fear.

Meanwhile, the supreme-level spirits, who would sometimes go decades or even centuries without seeing one another, seemed to be unbothered. They had already moved on to a different topic.

Ruri felt everyone around her was being *way* too cut-and-dried about this. Granted, Beryl was no better, leaving only a single letter in way of explanation.

However, Beryl's departure seemed to spark a change in Riccia as she also suddenly declared that she would be leaving the castle. This surprised Ruri greatly. Beryl had barely been gone a few days.

"Why? *Where* are you going? Are you planning to go on a journey like grandpa?"

Riccia remained nonchalant, despite Ruri's rapid-fire questions. "Oh, heavens no. You've got it wrong. I was thinking of moving into the house in the capital that you set up before."

Ruri was relieved to hear that her mother wasn't planning on going too far away, but she continued her questioning. "But why? Do you not like living in the castle?" She had prepared that house for Riccia and the rest of her family, so she'd expected that they would one day move there, but she was still curious.

"No, that isn't it. We've been treated very well here. Truly, it feels almost *too* good for us. But, you see, I've found my calling!"

"Calling?" Ruri had no idea what her mother was talking about, but she continued to listen.

"That's right. See, I looked into the clothing and apparel industry in this world, but everything is *so* stale! As a professional model, I *can't* let this pass! Women wearing dresses, men wearing pants—everyone's stuck in the Stone Age! I'm going to lead a *design revolution* in this world!"

Riccia had stated this so assertively that Ruri was taken aback. Still, it made sense given her mother's background. She was very particular about clothes. So particular, in fact, that Riccia had been busy trying to start up her own clothing line around the time Ruri had been summoned to this world.

The Nation of the Dragon King was home to many different races, so their selection of clothing designs trumped other nations, but it was apparently still too conservative for Riccia's tastes. She wanted to introduce new designs into the world, not just safe ones that everyone would like. She couldn't implement that while living in the castle, though. She said that she wanted to live in the house Ruri had prepared and open up her own clothing store in the town.

Ruri sighed and said, "Yeah, well, I won't stop you if that's what you want to do, but I think it's going to be tough to integrate a new piece of culture into society like that."

"That's where my power as a Beloved comes in. It's a better time than ever to utilize the Beloved brand. So don't worry, and leave it to me!" Riccia said, patting her chest in confidence.

Ruri decided to give up. She knew her mother wouldn't listen to anything she said. But at that moment, another problem came to mind.

"What about dad?" Ruri asked.

"He said he would come with me if I left the castle. He was offered a job to work here, so I suppose he'll be commuting."

"Well, I guess it's fine if dad is all right with it. Then that just leaves…" Ruri paused. Riccia was a Beloved, and you couldn't just compliantly let one out into the wild. "I'll talk it over with Jade-sama, so just hold on until then. Don't go off on your own like grandpa, okay?"

"Yes, I understand. I still have things I need to do here, after— Ah, Heat-chan!" Riccia called, waving her hand.

Ruri turned to see Heat walking with a woman on each arm. When he saw Riccia, however, he abandoned the women—most likely castle maids—did an about-face, and tried to run away. But Riccia quickly captured him. She wasn't going to let Heat slip away.

"Jeez, Heat-chan, I called your name," Riccia scolded, gripping his arm tightly.

Heat's mouth was twitching. He was normally so arrogant, and this rare reaction from him made Ruri acutely aware of how mighty her mother's influence was.

"U-Unhand me..." Heat stammered.

"But you *always* run away whenever you see me, Heat-chan," Riccia protested.

"Yes, because I don't want to *be* with you."

"*Ooh*? Mind *repeating* that?" Riccia trilled, approaching him with a sweet smile and a pensive glare.

"Eep!" Heat squeaked in terror. Yes, the same Heat who was always so pompous around Ruri was quaking in his boots.

"P-Please let me go..." Heat pleaded, his voice faint.

It was truly a sight to behold. Heat looked so pitiful with all the color drained from his face that even Ruri was feeling sorry for him.

"Mom, don't you have things to do? I'm going to go talk to Jade-sama, so why don't you get your business squared away?"

"Oh dear, you're right. I need to prepare so I can leave as soon as possible," Riccia replied, turning to Heat and planting a kiss on his cheek. "Toodles, Heat-chan."

Ruri watched in astonishment as her typhoon-of-a-mother walked away. Heat stood quivering in fear.

In Ruri's home country, a kiss on the cheek was a sign of great affection. Ruri was used to it since Riccia would kiss her like that almost every day, but Heat looked like he'd gotten hit with a missile.

"Heat-sama, are you okay?" Ruri asked.

"G-Good job, brat. I must commend you for getting rid of that woman."

"Uh, I mean, I didn't really do anything special..."

Ruri had no clue why Heat disliked Riccia so much, but there had been some sort of drunken spat between them during her wedding.

She couldn't get any information out of him as to why they'd fought, but she'd heard through the grapevine that it was about women.

Why a womanizer like Heat would get into a fight with a beautiful woman such as Riccia, Ruri had no idea. Heat's attitude toward her was abysmal, so perhaps he didn't treat *all* women with care just because they were women.

Ruri had also heard that after he upset Riccia, she'd dragged him off somewhere outside of the party grounds, which was where it had all gone downhill. Ever since then, Heat—the same spirit who acted arrogant even with the ruler of a nation like Jade—would start shivering whenever he saw Riccia.

When Ruri asked Riccia what in the world happened to him, Riccia had smiled sweetly and said, "Just a little discipline~!"

Not a single soul was brave enough to ask exactly *what kind* of discipline she'd administered outside of the public eye.

"Mom says she's going to leave the castle," Ruri told Heat.

"She's *what*?!" Heat exclaimed, his sallow face brightening up instantly. He let out a hearty laugh. "I see! I see! She's finally on her way out, is she?! Wa ha ha ha!"

As Riccia's daughter, Ruri felt conflicted about Heat's reaction. Was it really *that* much of a cause for celebration?

"Still, I need to talk to Jade-sama about it first."

"Then hurry on off to him, girl. And kick her out as soon as possible!"

"I would appreciate it if you didn't tell me to kick my own mother out…" Ruri retorted.

"Whatever you want. So long as I can be free from her vile clutches."

Ruri wanted to ask what had happened between them, but she was sure Heat would never talk.

Looking as if he was going to dance for joy at any moment, Heat had pushed Ruri on the back toward Jade's office. Once there, she knocked on the door and entered the room.

"Jade-sama, do you have a moment?" Ruri asked Jade, who was sitting with papers in hand like usual. Claus was by his side, helping with work, and Finn was standing near the door.

Jade's face went sugary sweet as soon as he saw her. "What's the matter, Ruri?"

"Well, you see… This time, my mom is saying that she's leaving the castle as well…"

"What?! Now it's Lady Riccia?!" Jade exclaimed.

Everyone in the room—Jade, Claus, and Finn—dropped their jaws in shock. That was understandable considering her grandfather had skipped town just a few days ago. It was hard for them to keep their calm when they heard that even Ruri's Beloved mother was also leaving.

"Oh, I said 'leaving,' but she's just moving to the house I had readied in the capital."

That house was close to Claus's residence, and many dragonkin inhabited that area, so it was the safest place aside from the castle.

Relief washed over Jade's, Claus's, and Finn's faces as they heard that added bit of news.

"I see. That mitigates the issue slightly, then," Jade said, sighing.

"I'm sorry. First my grandpa, then my mom."

"No, it's fine. It's fine as long as she's choosing to stay here in the capital. But why all of a sudden? Were they unhappy with life in the castle?"

"No, nothing like that," Ruri replied. "She said that she found her calling."

"Calling?" Jade repeated, question marks popping up in his head.

66

"She wants to open a business in the capital."

"Hmm, I see. That certainly would be hard to do in the castle," Jade said, tapping his finger on the desk. He pondered for a moment, then said, "Okay, then. Finn?"

"Sire!"

"I want you to permanently station several soldiers there as Lady Riccia's bodyguards. I'll leave the selection of the soldiers to you."

"As you wish, sire," Finn replied, bowing his head to his king's order.

"Claus, pick someone out to wait on her."

"Very well," Claus said, bowing his head as Finn did.

"If she wants to own a business in the capital, perhaps I should make preparations for that too…" Jade speculated.

"Oh, no! I couldn't let you do that much, so I'll handle it on my—" Ruri started, about to turn down Jade's offer, but Jade raised his hand and stopped her.

"No, Lady Riccia is a Beloved. I'd also like to prepare a place for her that's easy to protect from a security standpoint. And, of course, I'll take Lady Riccia's wishes into consideration."

Jade had spelled it out to her so plainly that Ruri felt she couldn't refuse without causing issues. So long as Riccia was a Beloved, she needed security detail. Even if Kotaro protected her like he did Ruri, she would still need security around her.

"She said that she'll leave once she's ready, so please let me know when things are ready on your end, Jade-sama."

"Very well. I'll get things ready at once. But what about Lord Kohaku?"

"She said dad is going to work at the castle and commute from the house."

"In that case, I will have a dragonkin escort him to and fro."

"That would be great!" Ruri exclaimed.

Ruri's father, Kohaku, would be working in the upper sectors of the castle. Also, considering that he was the spouse of a Beloved, he was allowed in the safe sectors—Sectors One through Five. It would be difficult for a human to traverse the upper sectors of the castle down to the town and then to their house on a daily basis. Those in the upper sectors usually had strong mana. They could commute with magic or fly, if they had wings like dragonkin. But for a human with no mana such as Kohaku, things were more difficult.

Ruri had been thinking of consulting Jade about this exact situation, so she was grateful that Jade himself had offered a solution. Otherwise, Kohaku would have to mountain climb to work. If he worked in Sector One, he would be above the clouds. He'd probably make it there by the time his shift ended.

"I think that my dad will be able to work with peace of mind," Ruri said.

Things wrapped up without a hitch thanks to Claus and Finn's quick work assigning the security guards and servants. Preparations were made in the blink of an eye, and Riccia left the castle in high spirits with Kohaku. However, for some strange reason, Riccia was dragging Heat away with her. Heat desperately pleaded for someone to save him, but Ruri and the others pretended not to see him.

Ruri clasped her hands together in prayer for Heat. She was certain that a daily routine of being pushed around by her mother was awaiting him. It was her hope that he would get a glimpse of how others felt being pushed around since he was always the one doing the pushing.

"Ruri, aren't you going to miss them?" asked Jade, his arm around her shoulder.

Ruri snuggled closer to him and replied, "Yes, a little. But...I can always go and visit them since they'll be in the capital, and dad will be coming to the castle every day."

"True. But whenever you go to see them, I'll be coming along with you," Jade said, showing his possessiveness even now of all times.

Ruri snickered. "Okay, let's go visit them together, Jade-sama."

The two of them smiled at each other. Jade slowly moved his face closer, and just when their lips were about to meet, Ruri quickly put her hand between their mouths.

"The tuning is not over yet," she stated.

"But the mood is just right for a kiss, isn't it?!" Jade protested.

"I don't think so. You *will* be keeping your promise," Ruri hurled at him, coldly and bluntly.

Reunion

With Beryl and Riccia now gone, the castle felt a little less lively than before. Ruri would be lying if she said that she didn't miss them, but it wasn't as if they were worlds apart. That thought helped console her a bit. Still, whenever she felt the loneliness of being away from family hit her, she turned into a cat and cuddled and nuzzled against Jade to her heart's content.

The reason she transformed into a cat was because she was too embarrassed to act that way as a human. Although she was anxious about showing signs of affection in human form, she had no qualms about it while in cat form. It made for an odd dynamic. Not that it mattered to Jade, though. He was thrilled that a fluffy cat was snuggling up to him, hungry for his affection. All in all, it was a win-win for both of them.

One day, as Ruri and Jade's trip to the Nation of the Spirit King drew nearer, Claus came to Ruri with a letter in hand.

"A letter for me?" she asked. She was in cat form and lounging atop Jade's lap.

"Indeed. Actually… I was hesitant to give it to you since it's from someone with whom you share quite a history. However, His Majesty said it would be wiser to let you make that decision."

Ruri looked up and met eyes with Jade, who nodded in confirmation.

"Whom is it from?" Ruri asked.

Claus hesitated for a moment before answering, "One of the people summoned to this world alongside you, Ruri."

"*Huh?!*"

Nadasha had brought Ruri, Asahi, and three of their middle school classmates to this world. Asahi and the others had been sent to a distant land called Idocrase, where they all lived as workers. The lord and lady of the land, Finn's parents, governed Idocrase. It was home to rich farmland said to be the Nation of the Dragon King's food storage. They had been sent there because Idocrase constantly lacked manpower due to the year-round harvesting. There were also many migrant workers there. Overall, it was a good environment for the four of them considering they no longer had anyone to turn to.

Quite some time had passed since they'd sent Ruri's former classmates away. Ruri rarely thought about them nowadays, instead choosing to leave them in the past and in her distant memory. Yet here they were now, attempting to contact her.

A tinge of dread rose in Ruri's heart. "*Don't tell me that it's from Asahi...*"

"No, it is from the other woman in the group," Claus replied.

Ruri was relieved to hear that. If it had been from Asahi, she probably would've burned it right then and there. No, she might just have read it out of fear. Either way, things were fine as long as it wasn't from Asahi.

"*I'll read it. Give me the letter, please.*"

"Here you go," Claus said, placing the letter on the desk.

At the same time, Jade took off her bracelet, and she reverted to human form. "If you're going to read it, it'd be better to do it in human form, right?"

"Thank you for that, Jade-sama," Ruri replied. She tried to get off of his lap, but his arm latched around her stomach from behind. She silently appealed to him, but he showed no signs of letting go. Conceding to his whim, Ruri remained where she was and opened the letter.

The letter itself was simple and short. Ruri's former classmate said that she wanted to see Ruri, that she was currently in the royal capital, and that…

"*Huh*?!" Ruri exclaimed.

Jade had been peeking over Ruri's shoulder at the letter, but he couldn't read it since it was written in Japanese. "What's the matter?" he asked.

"She's saying that she's getting married," explained Ruri.

"I see. That's joyous news."

"And it seems that she wants to meet me to give me a report."

"Well, Ruri, what do you want to do?"

Ruri thought it over for a bit. To be honest, she'd never really spoken to the girl. Nevertheless, the girl had left a lasting impression on Ruri because of all the hostility she'd shown due to Asahi's Bewitchment powers. Then again, once she awakened from the spell after Asahi's mana had been sealed off, the girl had apologized to Ruri, and Ruri had accepted it.

That was the extent of their relationship. They weren't necessarily on friendly terms, but they were among the rare few who hailed from the same world. Ruri thought it might be best to meet and talk with her. A part of her was also curious about Asahi's current status.

"I'll go meet her," Ruri decided.

"Then we'll arrange a meeting. Where is this person?" Jade asked.

"Looks like she's at an inn in the capital. The place she's staying is written on the back of the letter."

Since the note on the back was written in this world's language, Ruri showed it to Claus. Claus then immediately contacted the girl and set up a face-to-face meeting at the castle.

When the time came for the meeting, an unnecessary number of people stood inside the room to act as Ruri's security detail.

The girl stared at Ruri's face, curious as to what Ruri was getting at.

"That's why I hadn't remembered any of you at all."

"O-Oh, I see…" the girl stammered, her expression growing sullen. She was probably thinking that her visit had just been a nuisance.

Ruri continued, "What I mean is, you don't have to worry about it. Sure, a lot of stuff happened in the past, but I'm so happy now that I've forgotten all about it. So you should be happy too."

The girl lifted her head and gasped.

"Congratulations on your marriage," Ruri said with a smile.

Both Ruri and her former classmate realized that Ruri was able to say that because so much time had passed.

The girl smiled as tears rolled down her face. "Thank you…"

Handing the sobbing girl a handkerchief, Ruri asked, "How are the other two doing?" She was naturally referring to the two male classmates aside from Asahi.

"One of them said he wanted to save up and travel around this fantasy world someday. The other one appears to be in love with a rabbit-eared beast person who works with him. She doesn't seem to find the idea all that displeasing, so our coworkers are taking bets on when they'll be an item."

Laughter broke out between the two women.

"I'm glad to hear those two are enjoying this world as well," Ruri said.

"Yeah. By the way, are you going to ask about…Asahi-san?" the girl hesitantly inquired.

Ruri's expression turned sour. "Urk. A part of me wants to… and a part of me doesn't." She wavered, her curiosity coming and going. She hummed and pondered before asking, "Would you mind telling me?"

"Um, well, Asahi-san is… How do I put it? Um, Asahi-san…"

"Uh-huh, just as I expected. But I'm sure that she took a few licks from society and changed her ways. Well, even if she didn't make it that far, I'm sure she must have learned at least a *little* common sense, right?"

"She was pretty bad at first," the girl confirmed. "She wouldn't work, she would always complain, and she would always try to push her work onto someone else."

Ruri could picture all of that happening and more.

"But once the lady of the land blew a gasket and put her into a special curriculum, I'd say she's gotten a lot better."

"Special curriculum…?" Ruri looked up at Finn, who was standing next to her. "Erm, I'm sorry about that, Finn-san. It seems she's been causing problems…"

The girl looked confused by Ruri's apology.

"Finn-san is the son of the lord of Idocrase," Ruri explained.

This seemed to click with the girl. "The lord and lady of the land have treated me very well. I must extend my thanks," she said, bowing her head to Finn.

"Thank my parents. I didn't do anything," Finn replied, turning her down in his characteristically serious manner.

"Yes, that goes without saying. I am constantly grateful. It was the lady who suggested I go to the capital in the first place. She said that I should apologize in person if I felt *that* guilty. She even wrote a letter of introduction for me."

"So I see," Finn said, his intimidating aura somewhat softening.

"Anyway," the girl continued, "Asahi-san's learned a bit more common sense thanks to the lady's curriculum, but she is still, well, Asahi-san. She still has the same personality, so I don't think you should see her, Morikawa-san."

The image of Asahi merrily frolicking as they met again played in Ruri's mind. She put her fingers to her temple and said, "I appreciate the warning. I'll make sure not to see her even if I have the chance to go to Idocrase."

"I think that's a wise decision."

Ruri and the girl looked at each other and sighed. Right now, Asahi was tormenting Ruri's former classmates since they all worked in the same place. Ruri couldn't help but feel sympathy for them. Although it was probably too little, too late, she considered sending some token of appreciation to the lord and lady of Idocrase—especially the lady. Perhaps stomach medicine would do nicely.

"W-Well, anyway, I'm glad you're getting by all right. How long are you in the capital for?" Ruri asked.

"Since I've talked to you, I plan to go back to Idocrase after I do a little sightseeing around the capital. Actually, my fiancé is here with me."

"Huh?! He is?"

"He is. He actually told me that he would come with me here today, but I wanted to take responsibility myself, so he's waiting for me back at the inn."

"In that case, you better give him a *proper* reply," Ruri said in a playful tone.

Her former classmate smiled bashfully, her cheeks reddening, and nodded.

The two women had shared a much more engaging conversation than Ruri had expected, and the time had flown by in the blink of an eye until it was time to say farewell.

"Thank you for seeing me, Morikawa-san. I feel like a weight has been lifted off my shoulders."

"You're very welcome. Drop by if you're ever in the capital again."

Both girls knew that would be a very difficult thing to do. It wasn't easy for a mere commoner to meet Ruri, a Beloved, even if they were from the same place of origin. Jade and Claus probably only decided to show Ruri the letter because Finn's mother was acting as a go-between this time around. Nevertheless, Ruri wanted to see her again.

"Yes, most definitely," the girl said, nodding. "Either that, or let me know if you ever come to Idocrase, Morikawa-san. I'd like for you to meet the other two as well."

"All right, I'll send you a letter whenever that is."

In the end, both girls were able to part ways with smiles on their faces.

7 Journey to the Nation of the Spirit King

Ruri was at the harbor, ready to travel to the meeting of the four nations. Before her was a massive luxury liner, already docked. Ruri's mouth was agape at the sight of it.

"Whoa, incredible."

"It's a recently developed, state-of-the-art ship," explained Jade, standing next to her.

"We're not going to fly this time?" Ruri asked. The last time they went to the Nation of the Spirit King, Jade and the guards had transformed into dragons and flown there.

"We're not," Jade answered. "It's so that we can unveil this."

"You mean the ship?"

"It's a magic tool in the form of a ship based off of Lady Seraphie's witch knowledge. Using mana as its energy source, it can travel at speeds much faster than any conventional sailboat."

That reminded Ruri that Seraphie had asked her for a large quantity of magic stones not long ago. Ruri had given her a bucket full of them from the humongous pile in her pocket space, but she never would have guessed that Seraphie had made something this big and lavish out of them.

"This is going to revolutionize the ship industry," Jade declared. "Its speed is in a league all its own and will make it easier to travel between nations. I want to show this to the people of the Imperial Nation and the Nation of the Spirit King. Both nations have harbors that are invaluable trade points, and they possess their own naval fleets."

"You're going to sell them?" asked Ruri.

"To make a long story short, yes," Jade replied with a wicked face. He seemed to be implying that they would sell especially well with the Imperial Nation.

The Imperial Nation was mostly inhabited by humans. Few people there were capable of using magic, and they couldn't fly to the Nation of the Spirit King. They instead opted for long boat rides, which meant that traveling to the Nation of the Spirit King each year was an arduous process for them. Jade explained that if the Nation of the Dragon King had faster ships, the Imperial Nation would likely jump at the chance to buy them no matter how high the price.

While Ruri understood the logic, she thought it was rare for Jade to display a calculating, Amarna-esque fixation on money. But then Claus, who was also in attendance, whispered into her ear.

"Since that one time, we have received several letters from the Imperial Nation's nobles asking for a meeting with our Beloveds. Even His Majesty, who is usually so mild-mannered, is losing his patience with their persistent advances. That is why he plans to negotiate with them using this ship."

Jade's plan was to gouge the nobles at first, and once they faltered at the high price, he would offer to knock it down a little if they promised not to ask for a meeting with their nation's Beloveds ever again. He was positively fed up with the Imperial Nation's nobles by this point. The Beloveds in question were part of his family. This included Ruri, so she felt partially responsible.

It wasn't long before preparations were complete and Ruri boarded the boat—with Kotaro and Rin in tow, of course. Once she reached the deck, she realized that some sort of dispute was taking place in front of the stairs leading to the boat. She looked down to find Heat trying to board the ship, but Riccia, Ruri's mother, stopped him with a smile.

"I'm coming along too!" Heat yelled.

"Nuh-uh. You've got to be my model for my new clothes, Heat-chan."

"I said *no!*"

"Oh, come now, don't be so selfish," Riccia said, dragging Heat away from the ship.

Ruri pretended that she hadn't seen anything.

Riccia had started up a clothing business in a store Jade had graciously provided, and she'd been releasing design after design—all of them fresh and new for this world. Perhaps it was because she wore her own merchandise, but since she was a Beloved, her clothes were slowly starting to gain traction from a certain sect who loved new things.

While things were developing on that front, Riccia had apparently recruited Heat as the model for her menswear designs. It became clear why Riccia had taken Heat along with her when she left the castle. To Riccia's credit, though, she had great taste, so there was probably no one better to advertise her clothes than Heat. And considering that he could advertise the clothes *and* hit on every woman who entered the shop, it might have actually been his life's calling.

Riccia was satisfied with the situation, but Heat clearly did not like Riccia, hence his failed attempt to board the ship in order to get away from her. Ruri thought it was terrifying, even by her mother's standards, that she had Heat dancing in the palm of her hand.

After that little episode, Jade, Claus, and Finn boarded the ship. While Jade was away from the kingdom, the Nation of the Dragon King would be in the hands of the former king, Quartz, and the chancellor, Euclase. Both of them, as well as Seraphie and the Spirit of Light, had come to see everyone off.

Ruri waved to the crowd onshore as the ship started to set sail. Just as Jade had said, the ship was indeed faster than conventional sailboats. In addition to that, by hoisting the sails like a sailboat, it could go even faster with the added wind power. Ruri marveled at how storybook fantasy-like it was to have a boat powered by magic—a delayed observation given Ruri's time in this world.

Despite her awe, Ruri also worried if it was okay that Seraphie had shared Yadacain knowledge with the outside world. After all, the Yadacain witches had caused all sorts of problems with their Spirit Slayer magic. Ruri didn't have a stellar impression of them—Seraphie excluded, of course.

Fortunately, Claus helped dispel her doubts. "It is fine. Not a single trace of Spirit Slayer magic was used in the making of this."

That much was clear. Kotaro and the other spirits would never have allowed that to happen.

"The witches did not always use Spirit Slayer magic. The knowledge that Lady Seraphie provided was of the magic the original witches had used, free of any Spirit Slayer influences."

Basically, since the witches had used a different magic up until Spirit Slayer was created, they could make magic tools without it too.

"Ah, right," Ruri said, nodding. "Lydia told me that the second queen created Spirit Slayer, and the first queen was opposed to its creation, if memory serves."

Claus, who was hearing this detail for the first time, looked surprised. "Is that so?" he asked.

"According to Lydia, the first queen was killed by the next in line, the witch who created the Spirit Slayer magic. The first queen didn't want Spirit Slayer spreading to the outside world."

"Oh, so is *that* what happened?"

"Yes. Seraphie-san didn't know that either," Ruri explained, impressed at how spirits were essentially walking encyclopedias.

"Apparently, she was a great witch, so maybe she would have even been able to make an airplane."

"An air...plane?" Claus inquired.

"It's a vehicle from my world that zips through the skies."

"Oho, such useful innovations exist in your world, do they?"

Claus's jaw probably would have hit the floor if he saw one in real life. On the other hand, if anyone from Ruri's world were to see a dragonkin flying in the sky, their jaw would have undoubtedly fallen clean off.

Though airplanes were common in her world, traveling by boat wasn't particularly novel to Ruri. She was familiar with modern ships powered by engines, so she quickly became bored. The crew, on the other hand, only knew about sailboats. They all were curious about how this new ship moved.

Ruri knew that it moved by channeling mana through the magic stones acting as the power source, but only Seraphie knew the exact process. It was witch-exclusive knowledge. However, in the room where the magic stones were located, there was a giant magick ring—Ruri thought it was "magic," but according to Seraphie, it was actually called "magick"—carved out. The ship was running based on the writing on the magick circle, which was only decipherable to witches.

There were people suggesting that if this ship made a safe voyage, they should restore diplomatic relations with Yadacain and ask them for their witches' knowledge. Of course, it wouldn't be a one-sided deal. The Nation of the Dragon King would have to give something in return. That was what Jade and his aides were currently discussing, at least. None of it had anything to do with Ruri, and she wasn't supposed to interfere in political matters anyway, so she quietly left the room so as to not disturb them.

As Ruri stepped out onto the deck, the sea breeze pleasantly played with her hair.

"Mmm, that feels so good," she commented. Then she noticed someone squatting, their face pale. "Ewan, what's wrong? Not feeling well?"

"D-Don't worry about it. Just a little seasick… Urp!" Ewan moaned before holding his hands over his mouth.

"Are you all right?! Did you take any medicine?" Ruri asked, panicking.

"If I drink anything now, it's all coming out…"

Ruri gently rubbed Ewan's back. "Maybe you should lie down in your room, then?"

"I'm on lookout duty…"

"You can't carry out your duty like that. I'll ask the spirits to go on lookout for you, so go rest in your room," Ruri suggested.

After some slight hesitation, Ewan concluded that he was useless in his current condition and stumbled back to his room.

Once he was gone, Ruri asked the spirits for their help.

"Hey, guys? Tell me as soon as you see something happen."

The spirits gleefully replied.

"*Okay!*"

"*Got it!*"

Ruri had requested they keep a lookout, but she figured there'd be nothing *to* look out for on the open seas. Be that as it may, that all changed a few days later. At the time, Ruri was relaxing in her room.

It was going to take several days to reach the Nation of the Spirit King, no matter how fast the vessel went. No problems had occurred in the meantime, except a few people getting seasick. Other than that, the cruise was going swimmingly.

When they entered the waters of the Nation of the Spirit King, the ship switched to using wind power instead of mana. Mana was required to operate magic tools, but everyone would run dry of it in no time if they used it nonstop. They were distributing it in shifts, but operating a huge ship consumed a considerable amount of mana. Because of that, they would take breaks and operate it as a regular sailboat.

The voyage was going better than expected because operations had continued without a hitch, albeit at a leisurely pace. But just as everyone was resting easy and expecting to hit the Nation of the Spirit King's shores any moment, the sound of cannon fire suddenly echoed, nearly knocking Ruri out of her chair.

"W-What was that noise?!" Ruri asked, hearing a clamor outside her room.

"*Ruri~! There are weird guys here~!*" one of the spirits said.

"Huh? What weird guys?"

"*Guys with dirty beards~!*"

"*They're all scraggly~!*"

"*A whole bunch of them!*"

"I have no idea what you're talking about."

Ruri went outside to see what was happening and spied a large boat moored alongside their own.

"Huh? What? *What?!*" Ruri exclaimed.

As she panicked, people from the other ship started to march onto theirs. Just as the spirits had said, they were a bunch of men with unkempt, scraggly beards.

"Yeah, they definitely are scraggly," Ruri remarked.

"*Told you!*"

The weapon-wielding men ran amok on the ship's deck. As Ruri stood dumbfounded at the sight, Claus ran up to her. Despite what was happening, he wasn't panicking in the slightest.

"Ruri, please return to your room. It is not safe here," Claus said with an extremely calm—almost carefree—smile. He seemed detached from the battle ensuing around him.

"What is going on here?!" Ruri questioned, clearly the only one worrying.

"Oh, just a little pirate attack," Claus explained as though he were talking about a passing rain cloud instead of a ship raid.

Ruri's eyes were wide with shock. Once she heard that they were pirates, she looked up to see the big national flag of the Nation of the Dragon King hoisted high on their own mast.

She looked back to Claus, and with a grim expression, she said, "*Pirates?*"

"Yes," he answered.

"And they're attacking *this* ship?"

"Yes."

"*This* ship with *loads of dragonkin* aboard it?"

"Yes, this ship, indeed."

"So are they demi-humans with strength equal to dragonkin?"

"No, they seem to be regular humans."

After a moment, Ruri muttered, "Huh?! Are they idiots?"

Claus didn't refute it. In fact, his silence spoke volumes.

This ship was flying a flag with the crest of the Dragon King drawn on it, visible from even far away. It was pretty much declaring that the Dragon King was riding on this ship. The Dragon King, the world's mightiest dragonkin. Picking a fight with the strongest dragonkin around was nothing short of suicidal. Anyone who didn't know that was either just a moron or they had some sort of plan. Ruri wasn't sure which one applied to them, but judging by all the pirates laid out on the floor already, she had a feeling it was the former.

When she looked closer, she saw that Jade was at the front of the pack. He was knocking out pirate after pirate at a rate faster than the other dragonkin.

"No, I mean, they *have* to be idiots if they're attacking a dragonkin ship," Ruri asserted, unfazed now that she could tell from Claus's demeanor that everything was fine. Actually, she was starting to pity the pirates.

When the majority of the pirates were taken care of, Claus walked away to help with tying them up with rope.

"*Oh, Ruri!*"

"Huh?"

Ruri tried to turn around, but an arm reached out from behind her, restricting her movements. Another arm pointed a glinting dagger at her neck. She finally realized that one of the remnant pirates had apprehended her.

The homely bearded man shouted, "All right, listen up! If you don't want me to do anything to this girl, do what I say!"

He sounded like he was reciting tired lines from some two-bit performance, oblivious to the fact that everyone on the ship wanted him dead now. Jade's face was especially fearsome—enough to send a shiver down Ruri's spine, and she was on *his* side.

"Hey, mister, not to offend, but you might consider giving up now," Ruri suggested. She knew that Jade likely wouldn't forgive him now, but the sooner the bearded man gave up, the better. Judging by the anger-fueled, demon-esque Japanese hannya expression on Jade's face, she was not confident that the man would make it out alive.

Ruri then realized that the spirits were awfully quiet. She timidly looked to her side and, as she expected, she caught a glimpse of Rin and Kotaro scowling.

"Mister, you *really* ought to beg for your life…*fast*…"

"Say what?! Shut the hell up, ya li'l hussy! I'll kill you dead!"

"You try to give someone a friendly warning and this is what you get…" Ruri mumbled. Her kindness had been lost on the pirate.

Jade stood in front of them with his sword in hand and a face that would send grown men running for the hills. Even the rather dimwitted pirate was steadily turning paler in the face of Jade's intimidating aura.

"You scum. Touching Ruri is grounds for *death*. I'll cut those arms right off your pathetic body."

"Jade-sama, time out! Time out! Please calm yourself!" Ruri pleaded, attempting to stop Jade.

Jade then directed his anger at her as well. "Why are you stopping me?! I'm going to cut off that man's limbs, chop them up into fine strips, and chuck them into the sea for the fishes to eat."

"Yes, which is *why* I'm stopping you! I don't want front row seats to a *splatter show*!" Ruri desperately contested. She wasn't partial to getting drenched with blood.

"Enough of your goddamn yappin'! Shut the hell up!" the pirate said, bringing his dagger down on Ruri. However, since Ruri was constantly under Kotaro's protection, his dagger bounced off Kotaro's barrier and flew off into the distance.

As the pirate faltered, Ruri silently made her way to Jade's side. Jade hugged her tightly in relief. Meanwhile, the lesser spirits clung all over the bearded man.

"W-What the— I can't move my body!" he shouted. Evidently, he couldn't see spirits.

Rin followed up by making the seawater gush up like a pillar and swallow the man like a snake. The man choked, desperately struggling to breathe as the seawater enveloped his body. After a few seconds, he limply fell to the ground, unconscious. The water returned to the sea as if nothing had ever happened.

"You didn't k-kill him, did you?" asked Ruri.

"*Don't worry. I just made him lose consciousness,*" Rin replied, breathing heavily.

Kotaro, slightly unsatisfied with this punishment, casually stomped on the man's face with his front paw. Simply knocking someone out for attacking a Beloved was letting them off too lightly.

The rest of the pirates immediately lost their will to fight, and the dragonkin apprehended them one after another. Perhaps it was safe to say that this anticlimactic pirate raid had served as an excellent way for the dragonkin to kill some of their overabundant time.

Once everything was said and done, Ewan showed up looking as pale as a ghost. "What happened here?" he asked.

"Pirates attacked us. It's over now, though," Ruri stated.

"Oh, I see. Then I'm gonna go to sleep," Ewan declared. He wasn't fazed at all that there were pirates aboard the ship—a testament to the strength and trust of dragonkin.

"Yes, take care," Ruri said, smiling awkwardly.

After everything was squared away, the dragonkin wrangled the pirates into one spot so that they could hand them off to the Nation of the Spirit King later. The dragonkin seemed somewhat livelier thanks to that little bit of light exercise. Ruri couldn't help but feel sorry for the would-be bandits. Raiding a dragonkin boat, of all things, just showed that luck wasn't on their side.

One thing led to another, and eventually the ship hit the shores of the Nation of the Spirit King.

Arrival at the Nation of the Spirit King

Ruri and the others had finally arrived at the Nation of the Spirit King's harbor.

"We're here~!" Ruri exclaimed. Once she set foot on steady ground, she energetically stretched and took a big whiff of the foreign nation's air. Beside her, the tiny spirits mimicked her movements.

"It's spirits."

"You're right. And so many of them."

"It's a Beloved."

"That flag is from the Nation of the Dragon King."

The moment Ruri had stepped off the ship, the people around her had seen the gaggle of spirits serving her and immediately suspected that she was a Beloved. She was drawing quite a lot of attention, but she'd been called a Beloved for a long time now, so she had gotten pretty used to people gazing at her. And since they were all gazing with affection, not a disdainful look in the crowd, it was even less of a problem.

The Nation of the Spirit King's people were much more accustomed to Beloveds than other nations. And it wasn't just because they had a Beloved of their own either. It was because Lapis, the Beloved in question, would stroll around town without bodyguards. That would have been considered outrageous in the Nation of the Beast King, but here it was an everyday occurrence.

The people had accepted Lapis as a part of town life, even more so than the Nation of the Dragon King's people—all of whom Ruri thought were relatively amicable—had accepted her. That might have been because of the easygoing nature prevalent among the nation's citizens. In fact, they were so accustomed to Beloveds that the people who'd initially watched Ruri's arrival with surprise and curiosity began to lose interest and return to their tasks one by one.

Ruri and her group were getting set to head to the castle where the Spirit King was waiting. Envoys representing the nation had come to greet them. Jade, Claus, and the rest of the court began discussing what to do with the pirates they'd caught.

Ruri found herself with some free time on her hands, so she started to wander over to the open market at the harbor.

Jade noticed her doing so and called out, "Ruri, don't go too far."

"Yes sir, I know," replied Ruri.

"Ewan, escort Ruri."

"Very well, sire."

Ewan was still pale from his nasty bout of seasickness, but he seemed to have improved slightly after reaching dry land. That said, Ruri was highly concerned whether he would be able to serve as anyone's bodyguard looking as weary as he did. Although, she did have Kotaro and Rin by her side, two supreme-level spirits, so she had nothing to worry about. If anything were to happen to her, it would probably be something as benign as getting lost. Now that she was a little more conscious of her status as a Beloved, she wasn't going to worry Jade by moving out of his sight.

Ruri began to browse the open market. The fish and shellfish on display were somewhat different from that of the Nation of the

Dragon King. The marine life for sale were so strangely colored that it raised the question of whether they were even edible, but they drew Ruri's interest.

Perhaps the market people were used to Beloveds due to Lapis, because none of them were perturbed when Ruri came to their stalls. In fact, they addressed her like a neighbor. It also helped that her companion, Kotaro, was using the body of their nation's sacred beast.

"Lady Beloved, please come and try some of this. I assure you that it's delicious. This fruit is adored by Lord Lapis," said a female shopkeep.

"You don't say," replied Ruri.

"And how about you, O great sacred beast?"

"I'm not a sacred beast. I am the Spirit of Wind."

"Oh, dear. But you bear a resemblance to one. Well, care to partake?"

"Indeed, I will," Kotaro obliged.

They would stop at one shop, only for the neighboring shop to address them, prompting them to taste their goods as well—they were getting fed like animals at a petting zoo.

"Are you going to eat some too, Ewan?" Ruri offered.

"No thanks," Ewan said, covering his mouth and nose with a handkerchief. He was apparently still recovering from being seasick. The smell of the food was too intense for him right now.

Since he was still feeling unwell, they left Ewan alone and thoroughly perused all the stalls. Though the Nation of the Dragon King's capital had a harbor with a wide variety of products, the Nation of the Spirit King had its own assortment of uncommon delicacies. Ruri bought one thing after another that piqued her interest for souvenirs to take back to the Nation of the Dragon King.

Jade had given Ruri a large sum of money during their voyage—payment for all of the magic stones she'd provided so Seraphie could construct the ship. Originally, she'd given them to Seraphie so that she could make beast-transforming bracelets, but after Euclase forbade their production, the remainder of the magic stones and some extra Ruri had thrown in were put toward making the vessel. Ruri didn't mind how Seraphie used them since they were a gift anyway. She didn't feel any payment was necessary, but the magic stones had been invaluable in creating the ship-shaped magic tool, and they weren't easy to come by. She had practically been forced to accept the money, seeing as how the stones were far too valuable not to pay *anything* in return. Therefore, Ruri's pockets were now bursting at the seams.

The merchants witnessing Ruri's shopping spree suddenly perked up and frantically tried to get her to come to their stalls. It became a routine—taste and buy, taste and buy. She continued this pattern at every stall she visited.

As Ruri made her way through the market, she suddenly collided with someone. "Oh! Excuse me!" she immediately said. She'd been too focused on her food to pay attention to her surroundings.

The person she'd bumped into was a young man, slightly younger than Ruri, with brown skin and blond hair. His outfit was a tad different from the clothing of this nation. The Nation of the Spirit King's people wore East Asian garments—a mix between Japanese and Chinese designs—but the young man in front of her was clothed in Arabian-style garb. It immediately tipped her off to the fact that he was not from around here.

Despite Ruri's prompt apology, the man neither apologized nor responded. He just stared straight at her face. "Erm... Can I help you?" she asked.

The man gave her a friendly smile, flashing his pearly whites. Seeing his somewhat adorable smile, Ruri felt her heart skip a beat. The young man took her hand with both of his hands and squeezed.

"Huh?! U-Um…" Ruri stammered.

"What is your name?" he asked.

"Erm…"

"I'm Gibeon. And what is your name, beautiful?"

Feeling pressured by the sudden advances of this young man, Ruri blurted out in confusion, "R-Ruri."

"Ruri! What a beautiful name. It's almost like it was made for me. It's really cute."

Gibeon's flattery was reaching the point of exaggeration, but Ruri wasn't displeased. He was very suspicious, but she found herself charmed by his compliments. She blushed, feeling bashful, but Gibeon did not relent.

"How lucky I must be to meet such a lovely person here in a foreign land! Well, would you like to join me for a bite to eat?"

"I'm sorry. I have someone waiting."

Ruri peeked at Ewan. Gibeon looked at him as well—for all of a second—before he resumed staring at her.

"I can show you a better time than that boring-looking guy."

Ruri showed some resistance, moving away from Gibeon to give herself some much-needed space, but he quickly moved in and closed the distance.

"Or maybe I'm just not in the running for someone as cute as you?" Gibeon said, sounding suddenly sad and dejected.

Ruri panicked. "Huh? No, that's not it…"

Gibeon's face brightened. "Really? That fills my heart with joy," he said, his frown turning upside down so fast that he looked like a dog perking his ears and wagging his tail.

The display overwhelmed Ruri, filling her with emotions that she just couldn't put into words. However, Rin started shouting to bring her back to reality.

"*Oh, king! Ruri is cheating on you~!*"

"She's *what*?!" Jade exclaimed.

Although her group was within Jade's sight, they were standing a considerable distance away. Nevertheless, Jade's incredibly keen ears caught those words. He made his way over, glaring at Gibeon like his eyes could emit a death ray.

"Whoops, so *that* guy wasn't your boyfriend, but *that* guy way over there?" Gibeon, possibly realizing he stood little chance, took Ruri's hand, pecked the back of it, and walked off. "See you later, Ruri, my dear."

"Ruri!" Jade rushed over, scrubbing the back of her hand with a handkerchief. "Ewan, what were you even doing?! Weren't you standing by her side?!"

"Huh? My apologies, sire!"

Ruri felt a bit sorry for Ewan since he was still dealing with the aftereffects of his seasickness, but he had been assigned to be her bodyguard, and that was a fact.

Jade next directed his anger at Ruri. "And as for you, why didn't you offer more resistance?!"

"Aha ha… I'm sorry about that," Ruri replied, even though she'd been helpless in that situation. "It looks like I'm a sucker for puppy dog types. I made that discovery just now."

"Puppy dog types?" Jade asked, perplexed.

"Well, you know, cute guys who tickle my motherly instincts?" Ruri explained, referring to the exact vibe the young man had emanated. It was the same sort of soft spot she held for the spirits around her. She could never be firm with them if they looked at her with any hint of sadness.

"I see… I get it," said Jade.

"You get 'what,' now?" asked Ruri.

"You're essentially saying that you want a child as soon as possible. Leave it to me." Jade put his arm around her waist and pulled her close.

"No, wait, wait. I can't leave *anything* to you. How did you jump to that conclusion?!"

"You want to feel motherly, correct? Having children can solve that problem."

"I never said *one thing* about anything like that."

"I'll make sure that no other man ever lays their eyes on you again, so don't worry and give yourself to me," Jade said, holding onto her.

"Whoa! I'm sorry! I'm sorry! I won't say another word! I just lost myself a little bit back there!" Ruri asserted, flailing around in a panic. Nevertheless, Jade refused to let go and made her accompany him, putting her marketplace tour on hold.

Ruri knew what she'd said, but she'd been careless to say it in front of a dragonkin—the group that prided itself on mate supremacy. What she had meant as a light joke had not gotten through to Jade at all. She regretted saying it, and she vowed to never joke like that ever again.

All jokes aside, Ruri was a bit curious about the young man from before. Telling Jade seemed like a recipe for disaster, so she whispered it to Rin and Kotaro, who were both by her side.

"Hey, wasn't there something strange about that person?" Ruri asked.

"Oh my, you thought the same, Ruri?"

"You too, Rin? What about you, Kotaro?"

"Indeed. I too was quite curious."

97

"I'm not sure how to put it. It was like he had no presence," Ruri elaborated. "I didn't realize that he was near me until I bumped into him. Also, Ewan and the other bodyguards were around, but no one came to help."

No one by Ruri's side had come to intervene even though a suspicious character was getting so close to her. Ewan was definitely out of sorts, but he wasn't incompetent enough to let that slip by. Given how surprised Ewan had looked, it was like he'd only noticed Gibeon's existence after Jade had come over.

"*We noticed him, but no one else did. It was like everyone finally noticed only after I called out to the king. I feel like I've seen something similar to that in the past...*" Rin said, tilting her head. She looked like she was trying to remember but failing to do so.

Kotaro seemed similarly troubled. "*I am stymied myself. It might be good to tread carefully, just in case. Neither of us sensed any hostility from him, so we left him alone at first, but I'm still slightly concerned.*"

Kotaro then ordered several of the nearby spirits to chase after the young man. The spirits did as they were told, but they returned not even a few minutes later.

"What happened?" Ruri asked.

"*We lost sight of him!*"

"*He went somewhere~!*"

"Huh?"

Ruri looked at Kotaro, as if to ask if a spirit could even lose sight of someone. Both Kotaro and Rin grimaced.

Rin commented, "*My, he is getting more suspicious by the minute.*"

"*If he can escape the eyes of a wind spirit, then he's no ordinary fellow,*" added Kotaro.

"*This calls for some serious investigation, don't you think?*"

"*Indeed. If we wait until something happens to Ruri, we'll be too late.*" Kotaro was as much of a worrywart as Jade.

"But I should be fine since you have your barrier around me at all times, right?" Ruri asked.

"No, it'd be too late if we wait until something arises. I'll mobilize all the spirits in the Nation of the Spirit King's capital."

"Huh? Are you sure about making such a big move?"

This wasn't the Nation of the Dragon King; it was the Nation of the Spirit King. Ruri was worried about acting without permission on someone else's land, but spirits weren't bound by man's national borders in the first place. Kotaro had already finished giving out the order before she even had a chance to stop him.

"You sure are overprotective, Kotaro."

"I cannot fall behind the curve and allow you to face peril like with the Church of God's Light. I will protect you."

Not only was Kotaro a faithful canine, but he acted like a stud. If Ruri wasn't married to Jade, her heart probably would've started fluttering. She hugged Kotaro's soft and fluffy body with all of her might, thanking him for his efforts.

9 The Three Beloveds

Ruri and the others rode in a carriage provided by the welcome party, and it wasn't long before they made it to the castle. The castle, floating atop a lake, was just as captivating and beautiful as ever. This was Ruri's second time seeing it, but its beauty moved her no matter how many times she looked at it.

"Those from the Nation of the Beast King and the Imperial Nation arrived not too long ago, so everyone is assembled," said a man from the welcome party.

"I see. I thought we left early, but I suppose we took too much time," Jade replied.

As the two men conversed with one another, Ruri stood at the castle's entrance with her mouth agape. Her eyes were transfixed on a certain something sitting there.

"Kotaro is here…" she murmured.

Yes, there was Kotaro, adorning the entrance. Of course, it wasn't the current Kotaro. It was the body of a large boar-like magic beast that Kotaro had used before he acquired his current body. It was sitting up straight, looking regal and eye-catching.

"Why is this here?" Ruri asked, confused.

The person from the Nation of the Spirit King explained, "This was left behind by the Spirit of Wind. We struggled with how to dispose of it since, even though it was a magic beast's body, it was a *special body* used by the great Spirit of Wind.

We couldn't just dispose of it like any old beast, so we decided to have it stuffed and placed at the entrance for all to see. Of course, we obtained the permission of the great Spirit of Trees."

"Right. Is that so?" Ruri remarked.

Kotaro had mentioned that he'd left his previous body here since it was dead weight. Ruri had worried that it would end up on a dining table; she never would have expected that she'd see it again, especially stuffed and on display. She had mixed feelings about it, but she decided to accept it since they were taking good care of it as an outdoor art installment.

"You all must be weary after your long trip. I shall lead you to your rooms."

Since they would be meeting the Spirit King and the people from the other nations tomorrow, they were shown to their rooms so that they could relieve their fatigue.

The room made up for Ruri was actually Jade's, as if it were a matter of fact. Granted, it wasn't a problem since they were husband and wife now. Actually, they'd been sleeping in the same room even *before* they were married.

Nothing had felt strange about it at first since they met when she was masquerading as a cat. But they continued to sleep in the same room even after Jade learned that she was a human—which was odd in retrospect. However, given the fact that no one called it into question, it was probably every vassal's wish at that point to make Ruri the Dragon Queen—with Ruri being none the wiser.

Though it had all worked out because Ruri had accepted Jade as her mate, what would have happened if she had gone with *someone else*? Considering how clingy and touchy-feely Jade was now, she was too afraid to even picture it. He would likely make whoever it was disappear—permanently. After all, he *was* the Dragon King, a man with power and authority in no short supply. He could easily get rid of one person. Surely Ruri wasn't the only one who was relieved that their love was mutual.

While Ruri was relaxing with Jade, Kotaro and Rin came into the room. They'd apparently gone to say their hellos to the Spirit of Trees.

"Welcome back," Ruri greeted them.

"*Indeed,*" replied Kotaro.

Rin added, "*Good to be back!*"

Kotaro and Rin took the couch across from Ruri and Jade.

"*Ruri, it seems I still cannot track down the man you met in the market,*" Kotaro reported.

"Not even you can find him, Kotaro?" Ruri asked in astonishment.

"*Nope.*"

"What the heck?"

The fact that not even Kotaro, a supreme-level spirit, could find him made Ruri all the more curious about who this man was. But then an unpleasant thought crossed her mind.

"You don't think that *Spirit Slayer* is in use, do you?" asked Ruri.

"*No. If that were the case, either Rin or I would have noticed when we met him. This is a different matter.*"

"Then what could it be, I wonder."

"*That I do not know. I will just have to keep looking.*"

"Okay."

Jade, who had been listening to Ruri's conversation, looked puzzled as he asked, "What are you all talking about?"

"About the man that I met today," Ruri replied, explaining to Jade how suspicious the young man named Gibeon had been.

"Yes, that sounds suspicious indeed. Come to think of it, that outfit of his looked to be the native garb of the Nation of Iolite."

"The Nation of Iolite?"

"A land that fell to ruin not too long ago," Jade explained. "A neighboring nation attacked Iolite and assimilated it into their own, thereby eliminating its name. Judging by his clothes, I would assume that he has close ties to the Nation of Iolite."

"Huh, you don't say…"

"But I don't know exactly *what* those ties may be," Jade added.

Ruri turned to Kotaro. "Maybe you should just leave him be?"

"*No. At this point, I will not be satisfied until I find out who he is,*" Kotaro replied, showing his stubborn side.

The next day, the kings of the four nations and their Beloveds assembled. Jade escorted Ruri, who was dressed more lavishly than usual, into the room that acted as their meeting place. The other participants were already in attendance.

Once Jade stepped through the door, someone Ruri was familiar with came rushing toward him. It was Celestine, the Beloved of the Nation of the Beast King. "Master Jade!" she called.

Ruri slipped between Celestine and Jade as Celestine tried to cling to Jade's arm. Ruri held her arms out wide and blocked the way.

Celestine frowned. "Lady Ruri, you're in the way!"

"Naturally. That is my intention. Jade-sama is my husband now, so I ask that you not get too handsy with him!"

"I still do *not* accept that as fact!"

"What are you talking about?! You were at the wedding!"

"Aaah, aaah, I can't hear you!" Celestine said, covering her ears.

"Why are you acting like a *child*?!"

"I said I don't accept it and I mean it. That was surely a hallucination. I am all but certain it was."

103

"You are being *such* a sore loser. Why not just give up and face facts already?"

"Never!"

Jade and the Beast King, Arman, could only watch in dismay as Ruri and Celestine bickered. Instead, it was the Imperial Nation's Emperor, Adularia, who spoke.

"You two there, I know you're quite chummy with one another, but would you mind taking your seats already?"

"Lady Adularia, we are by *no means* 'chummy,' as you so put it," Celestine corrected her.

Though Ruri and Celestine were the only ones who didn't realize it, from an outsider's perspective, they looked like they were just friendly ribbing each other.

Now that the bickering was finished for the time being, everyone settled into their seats. A silent tug-of-war began between the two ladies over who would sit next to Jade. Without any recourse, they sat in the seats on either side of him, sandwiching him in the middle.

"Now then, let's begin," Awain, the Spirit King, said. He signaled for a meal to be carted in.

The food in the Nation of the Spirit King wasn't as heavily seasoned as the food in the Nation of the Beast King. Here it was lightly seasoned and mainly used broth made from fish and seaweed— things that Ruri was very familiar with.

While this food suited Ruri's palate more so than the Nation of the Dragon King's, she thought it might be a little lacking for the Nation of the Beast King's two representatives. However, when she looked closer, she could see that Celestine and Arman's food was a darker color than hers, implying that their meals had been tailored to their tastes.

Ruri talked among the others and enjoyed the seafood cuisine, similar to traditional Japanese kaiseki-ryori. The conversation was mostly all small talk about topics that even she, who didn't have a clue about politics, could follow.

The rulers were more focused on the ship that Jade was so confident in. Awain and Adularia reacted favorably to the prospect of a ship that could travel faster than any before.

Then, as if on cue, Jade began to speak about the topic that had been on his mind.

"The Nation of the Dragon King had three Beloveds—Ruri and two members of her family. The nobles of the Imperial Nation took exception to that, and once Ruri's grandfather learned of it, he left on a journey so as to mitigate any trouble. He took the supreme-level Spirit of Earth with him."

Jade shot a stern look at Adularia.

Adularia held her head and let out a deep sigh. "What a fine mess."

The palpable anguish in the ruler's voice made Ruri feel she should do some damage control. "Oh, please don't worry about it. Grandpa isn't the type of person who stays in one place for very long anyway."

Adularia shook her head. "No, the blame is squarely on us. I reprimanded the whole lot of those foolish noblemen, but it seems that I was a little too late."

"As a result of this, our nation has lost one Beloved," Jade continued. "Although it is not allowed to keep any Beloved against their will, the Imperial Nation's nobles are clearly to blame here."

"That's right. It's been a headache for me as well. I have more idiots in my court than I ever expected. Believe it or not, that's them keeping things *civil*."

"Which brings me to my point," Jade said. "Allow me to strike a deal with those fools for the ship."

Adularia's eyes widened. "Why?"

"It's a magic tool that's a *ship*. I want them to understand that it is indeed rare and valuable. It's also something that I can't easily give away."

Adularia nodded. His suggestion had confused her at first, but she smirked deviously, quickly picking up on what Jade was implying. "Hmm, now I get it. You're going to use the ship as bait to silence the nobles. Very well. Our nation's prestige is on the line. I will pressure them so that they make sure the dealings for this new ship with your nation succeed at any cost."

"I'm glad we see eye to eye on this matter," said Jade, he and Adularia grinning slyly at one another.

Seeing that matters were settled, Awain interjected, "But is the Beloved who left going to be all right? They are a human, aren't they? It would be terrible if something happened to them. Shouldn't you keep a guard detail on them?"

"Well, you see… Andal is with them, apparently," Jade said, glancing at Arman.

Andal was not only Claus's father, but also Arman's father. That was probably the reason Arman grimaced in disgust when he heard Andal's name.

"That rotten old man is with him?" Arman asked.

"Oh, well, that explains things. I suppose that's a good enough reason not to be worried. Andal is a seasoned traveler. He also has the Spirit of Earth with him," Awain said, convinced that things were fine—contrary to what Arman thought.

"So I see. He'll be fine because Andal is with him, then," Adularia surmised.

Once their meal was over, and Ruri was looking forward to dessert, Arman turned his attention to Celestine.

"Celestine," Arman called.

"Lapis," Awain said in similar fashion.

The two of them stood from their seats as if they knew what this implied.

Ruri watched in confusion, but Jade filled her in. "Ruri, Awain has prepared after-dinner tea for all of you in another room. You should go there with Celestine and Lapis."

Ruri immediately picked up on the hint. Awain was saying that the top brass of all the nations were about to start a complex conversation. Meaning that any Beloveds, who were unable to interfere in political affairs, needed to vacate the meeting hall.

"Right, then," Ruri replied. She copied the other Beloveds and stood up from her seat, following them as they left.

Jade then called out behind the group in a low, threatening tone, "Lapis, if you lay a *finger* on Ruri... Well, you know the consequences."

"Um, yes sir!" Lapis replied, nodding repeatedly before rushing out the room in fear. Ruri smiled awkwardly and followed behind him.

In the room they were led to, there were more sweets than they could possibly eat, and once they sat down, tea was served. The tea had a vibrant pink hue, but it tasted like green tea, sending mixed signals to Ruri's brain. It was delicious, nonetheless. The astringent tea went well with the sugary sweets.

As Ruri got swept up in the sugar rush and munched away, Celestine sharply commented, "You're going to get fat, you know."

"Grk!"

Ruri had been with Jade in his office a lot as of late. As a result, she hadn't gotten much exercise, so she had been worried about the extra weight she'd put on. She shot Celestine a glare, Celestine's amazing figure catching her eye, before she silently returned to nibbling on her plate of sweets.

"Oh, don't let it get to you. You should eat whatever you want. Why, eat until you become so unsightly that Master Jade tosses you by the wayside."

"Jade-sama would never toss me by the wayside because of that!" Ruri confidently declared.

Celestine gave Ruri the once-over and then sighed heavily. "Aah... Why did Master Jade pick this welp of a girl instead of me? I fail to understand."

"That is *so* rude! You have some nerve saying that right in front of my face."

Celestine, for whatever reason, was merciless when it came to Ruri. Part of that might have been because they were romantic rivals, but it also felt as though Celestine was being more herself because they were both Beloveds.

"By the way, are you finished tuning yet?" asked Celestine.

"No, not yet," replied Ruri.

"I see. Not yet, are you?" Celestine repeated, giving Ruri a suggestive stare.

"W-What is it?" Ruri asked, now on guard.

"Nothing. I was just thinking that maybe I can make something happen before your tuning is complete."

"You *cannot*!"

Celestine's undying love for Jade pushed Ruri past the point of anger and toward a weird form of respect.

As they continued their conversation, a woman came into the room bearing fresh tea. Once Lapis saw her, he knelt in front of her and said, "I've fallen in love at first sight. Be my wife." It was the same old routine. Both Ruri and Celestine just rolled their eyes.

"It makes your head hurt to think that he is a Beloved as well, doesn't it?" Ruri commented.

"It's a sickness. An incurable sickness that not even dragon's blood can help alleviate. Leaving him be is the best option," replied Celestine.

"Did you fall prey to Lapis once before as well, Celestine-san?"

"Yes, when I first met him. I quickly shot him down by telling him that Master Jade is everything to me."

"You're pretty persistent yourself, you know, Celestine-san."

"Why, yes, of course I am. For there is *always* that one-in-a-million chance," Celestine said with a sweet smile, not a hint of resignation.

Cheater Detected?

As the Beloveds sat and enjoyed their tea, the top brass of the four nations came into the room and joined them. It seemed their discussion had ended.

Jade naturally gravitated to Ruri's side. Once he was settled, he brought a perfectly bite-size sweet to Ruri's mouth.

Celestine glared—hard. Pretending not to see her disdainful gaze, Ruri accepted the feeding custom exclusive to dragonkin mates, partnerial allofeeding.

"Jade, we have dinner after this. Don't feed her too much," warned Awain.

Jade continued to gallantly serve Ruri, as if the warning never reached his ears, bringing food to her mouth.

Awain gave up on Jade and turned to Ruri instead. "Tomorrow, we'll be holding a party to welcome the rulers and Beloveds. As for your outfit for the occasion, we can prepare one for you. What do you say?"

"By that, do you mean the clothes of the women working in the castle?" Ruri asked.

"Those are just the servant uniforms. We will prepare something *much* more lavish for your party wear. I'm sure they will look splendid on you."

The women of the Nation of the Spirit King wore kimonos, with the layered cloth tied together in front with an obi sash, so you could say their clothes looked like that of a tennyo—a celestial being with elaborate robes. It was a mix of Japanese and Chinese styles.

The flowing kimono made out of soft material piqued Ruri's curiosity. "Wow, I'd like to wear one. Will you also be wearing one, Celestine-san?" she asked with hopeful eyes.

"Huh? *Me*?" Celestine faltered, eyes wide from the unexpected question. "Well, let's see… What should I do?"

Seeing that Celestine was being indecisive, Jade remarked, "I think it'd look quite pretty on you, Celestine."

"Then wear it I shall!"

Jade's words were literally an order from the top. Celestine couldn't possibly say no after hearing them from Jade's mouth. And it seemed that Jade had made that comment knowing this would happen, because he smirked in satisfaction.

"This is the first time you've ever worn our nation's clothing, isn't it, Celestine?" Awain asked. "I'll have them readied immediately. The others will surely be pleased to see you two Beloveds in our nation's garb."

"I'm looking forward to it!" Ruri said enthusiastically.

With that settled, everyone was about to return to their rooms until dinner. But just then, a soldier who'd been standing guard outside came in.

"Excuse me for intruding on your gathering. Lady Spinel of the House of Morga wishes to seek an audience with His Majesty the Dragon King. What should I tell her, sire?" the soldier asked Awain.

Awain looked at Jade and asked, "You two are acquaintances?"

"No. Who is this 'Spinel'?"

"There is a group of nobles here in the Nation of the Spirit King who lead the other nobles. They're called the House of Morga, and they have supported the nation since the days of old. Spinel is the daughter of that family. So you *don't* know her, Jade? Well, I suppose that makes sense; she's apparently quite frail and hardly ever attends social gatherings. Even I only have a faint recollection of what she looks like. That being said, why would she want a meeting with you?"

"I don't know. But I'll meet her and find out. Mind if I let her in?"

Jade looked to the Emperor, the Beast King, and the Beloveds for permission. Each of them nodded in approval. This girl wanted a meeting so badly that she would interrupt a luncheon for the leaders of the four mightiest nations. Everyone figured that she must have had some adequate reason for doing so, and their curiosity as to what it was got the better of them.

The Spirit King ordered the soldier to let Spinel into the room. Spinel entered shortly after. She was a young girl—slightly younger than Ruri and Celestine—with loose wavy hair that was pulled half up. She was an adorable maiden as soft and sweet as cotton candy, with doe eyes that evoked one's natural desire to care for and protect her.

Spinel knelt in front of the top brass, crossing her arms in front of her chest and lowering her head. This curtsy was the greatest show of respect in the Nation of the Spirit King, and she performed it with fluid elegance. As the daughter of the head nobles, her conduct was exemplary.

"I am Spinel, daughter of the House of Morga. Excuse me for intruding on your function."

"Intruding is right. This may be happening because the other rulers and Beloveds allowed it, but you *do* realize how rude your actions are, do you not?" Awain chided. He looked at Spinel with his sharp eyes that would make a child burst into tears.

"I am aware. A thousand apologies, sire…" Spinel replied.

Spinel looked less afraid of Awain and more depressed. Seeing her like that was enough to stir even Ruri's innate desire to care for and protect—something that rarely happened when she saw a fellow girl.

Spinel had tugged at Arman's heartstrings, and he stepped in to mediate. "C'mon, there's no harm, is there? You know that old men shouldn't go scaring kids."

"Arman, I resent you calling me 'old.'"

"Oh, come off it," Arman snapped back. "You've lived the longest out of anyone here. In fact, you're older than my dad, so what the hell do you 'resent'?"

Adularia nodded emphatically in agreement.

As Awain sat there at a loss for words, Jade tried to get the conversation back on track. "That aside, what business brings you here to see me?" he asked her.

Spinel's expression brightened like a flower blooming. Then she stared at Jade and blushed.

"What business? That sounds so cold and distant. The reason I am here is obvious, is it not? I am here to see you, Master Jade," Spinel said with familiarity.

Of course, there would be no way that one could live in the Nation of the Spirit King and *not* know of the Dragon King, who ruled one of the allied nations. Yet she seemed to be implying that she didn't just know Jade, but that their relationship extended further.

Jade, on the other hand, said that he had no idea who she was.

Everyone else started contemplating about this discrepancy.

"You see, I am finally of age," Spinel explained.

"Okay…" Jade replied. He looked like he wanted to ask what that meant. A stranger, who he'd never met before, coming into their adulthood had nothing to do with him. But he patiently waited for her to explain. However, the next words out of her mouth made Jade and everyone else gape at her.

"You promised that you would marry me once I became of age, did you not? I have finally become an adult, so I can now become your wife, Master Jade. As I waited with bated breath for the day you would come for me, I received word that you were at the royal castle, so I rushed over."

Not a single person in the room uttered a word.

Ruri shot a displeased glare at Jade. "Jade-sama…"

"W-Wait, that's not right! I don't remember making *any* such promise!" Jade desperately refuted, sensing the contempt coming from Ruri's eyes.

Spinel interrupted him, driving her point home. "I have waited so long for you, Master Jade. I would call out for you every night as I looked at your portrait. I even have my dress for the wedding all prepared."

Spinel didn't look like she was lying. Because of that, eyes of doubt fell upon Jade from all directions.

"Wait! *Ruri* is my wife. And I've never even met you before!" Jade exclaimed.

"Is that true?" questioned Ruri.

"*Absolutely*!" Jade affirmed, squeezing Ruri's hand tightly as if to say that he wasn't going to let her run away from him.

"Then, let's say, for example…you made her a lighthearted verbal promise while she was still a child, thinking nothing of it?"

"I have *no* recollection of that!"

Adularia, amused, watched Jade panic until she turned to Spinel and asked, "Did you really make that promise with Jade?"

"Yes, I did," Spinel answered.

"When did he tell you that?"

"When I was a child. He said that he would come for me when I was of age."

All eyes fell upon Jade…again.

"Y-You're wrong!" Jade cried.

Celestine then stood up. "Your name is Spinel, right?"

"Yes. And you are?"

"I am the Beloved of the Nation of the Beast King," Celestine answered. She hadn't given her proper name probably because she didn't plan on letting the girl address her by it in the first place. "Master Jade already has someone, and that is *me*. I don't know *or* care about your little game of house, so give up and scurry on home."

"No, wait, wait. *You've* got it wrong too!" Arman quickly declared.

Celestine, however, didn't care. "You will *never* become Master Jade's spouse."

Spinel made a huffy expression. "You have no right to tell me that!" she yelled just before gasping in some sort of realization. She looked at Celestine with pity and said, "Aah… Master Jade must have been playing games with you. I mean, he already had someone, and it was *me*. I'm sure he couldn't wait for me to come of age, so he used someone else to fill the gap that I left. I feel so sorry for you."

"Well, I never!" replied Celestine, shocked.

She wasn't the only one shocked either. Everyone else aside from Spinel was surprised. No one expected anyone to hurl such language at a Beloved. Not only that, but she'd been so casually rude to Jade as well. Awain reacted the most strongly, though; he went completely pale.

After all, it was a subject from his own kingdom saying such things to a Beloved and the ruler of another nation.

"Spinel!" Awain reflexively snapped at the girl.

Spinel looked at him with a vacant stare, completely clueless. "Yes? What is it, sire?"

"What you just said was extremely rude to both the Beloved and Jade. Apologize *at once*."

"Huh?"

"Also, Jade already has a spouse that he shared a marriage ceremony with. You *cannot* be Jade's spouse."

"What are you talking about? I *am* Master Jade's spouse."

"Jade…" Awain said, looking at the man in question to hint that he should help the lost girl firmly understand the situation.

Jade took Ruri's hand and stood in front of Spinel. Spinel gleefully reached out for him, but he embraced Ruri before her hand could reach him. She looked at Jade, then at Ruri, and then back at Jade with a confused expression.

Jade then explained, "I only have one partner for life, and she is standing right here—Ruri. There seems to be somewhat of a misunderstanding, but I have *not* come to make you my spouse."

Spinel's eyes widened. She placed her hands over her mouth and muttered in disbelief, "It can't be. It can't be…"

"If you understand, then you should leave. I will be talking with the head of the House of Morga about this matter," Awain said, using his eyes to signal to the soldiers waiting in the wings.

The soldiers quickly moved and took Spinel outside. Once she'd left the room, the tension immediately disappeared.

"I'm sorry, Jade, Ruri, and you as well, Celestine," Awain apologized.

"You needn't worry about me," Jade assured him, "but I think that sort of attitude is dangerous to take with Celestine, knowing full well that she's a Beloved."

"Agreed. That whole ordeal was chilling even for *me*. You have to forgive me, Celestine," Awain pleaded.

"No need to apologize, Master Awain. I was more surprised than angry since I've never had anyone speak to me in that manner before."

The others present probably shared Celestine's thoughts.

Awain added, "They likely don't know much of the world since they don't participate in social gatherings. I'll speak to the House of Morga in any case."

"Yes, please do so," Celestine replied.

That matter was now settled, but Arman dragged up the *other* matter.

"Still, Jade, you're a cad. Never would have guessed you'd mess with that girl," Arman said with a grin, totally amused by the situation.

"I did *not*! I have no recollection of anything of the sort!" Jade insisted.

"But it happened when she was a child, didn't it? You probably just forgot because it went down so long ago, right? Poor little thing. She said she was waiting for you to courageously come and get her. What are you going to do, Ruri?"

Ruri covered her face with her hands. "I can't believe that you were having an affair, Jade-sama! No, actually, since I came into the picture afterward, have *I* been the one cheating?!"

"Hold on! That's not it at all!"

"How could you do something as dishonest as promising to marry someone, then forgetting?!" Ruri exclaimed, her shoulders trembling slightly.

"I told you that isn't what's going on here, didn't I?! You're the *only* one for me, Ruri!"

Ruri watched Jade panic through the gaps in her fingers. He was so shaken up that Ruri couldn't help but laugh.

Hearing her chuckle, Jade frowned in displeasure. "Ruri..."

Ruri gave up and took her hands away to reveal that she was giggling instead of crying.

"Teasing me like that is so mean-spirited," Jade grumbled.

"But seeing you get so shaken up was so much fun, Jade-sama. So...you really don't remember making that promise?"

Jade regained his composure, thought about it, and shook his head. "I don't."

"Then how did she end up with that idea?" Ruri wondered.

"Because the girl is mistaken. I have no recollection of saying something like *that* to a child. Do I look like the type to say that?"

"Well, no, to be honest. The Beast King and Lapis, on the other hand?" Ruri said, peeking over at Arman and Lapis.

"Hey, what do you mean by that, Ruri?" Arman questioned.

"You should know *very well* what she means," Celestine interjected, shutting Arman down. "It *is* your daily routine by now, Master Arman."

"If it were me, I would marry them without that 'after they become an adult' stipulation!" Lapis asserted in an oddly boastful manner, but everyone ignored him.

"Since the House of Morga will also be attending tomorrow's welcome party, I think you should be careful, just in case," Awain suggested. "We can only hope what just happened was enough to convince her..."

"Spirit King? Where I'm from, that's what we call a 'red flag,'" Ruri said with a tinge of anxiety.

Unfortunately, that anxiety would soon become a reality.

11 Disorder before the Welcome Party

The next day—the day of the welcome party—Ruri leisurely got out of bed and had breakfast. When she woken up, she had noticed that Jade wasn't next to her. According to the spirits, he had left the room before she awakened. Apparently, it was so that he could have breakfast with the other leaders. Ruri wished that he had woken her up while he was at it, but she had a hunch that the group would be discussing politics—something that they couldn't do in front of her.

When she asked the person who brought her breakfast about the welcome party, they responded that it would be held in the evening, meaning she would have free time until then.

Although she was told that she could do whatever she wanted, Ruri had no idea what to do. She couldn't very well go outside, so she decided to just stay in her room. However, she quickly became bored.

She looked out her window to see the delightful blue sky spread out before her. "Maybe I should go soak in some rays," she said.

"*Good idea!*"

"*Yay!*"

"*I'm comin' too!*"

Ruri took the spirits, who were pleased by the idea, out of the room. There she saw Ewan standing watch at the door.

"Huh? You're here Ewan?" she asked.

"Of course I am. I have to serve as your bodyguard, after all."

"Thank you," Ruri said, talking to the other dragonkin guards there as well.

"Going somewhere?" Ewan inquired.

"Yep, I'm going to go sunbathing since it looks so nice outside."

"Then I'll come along with you," Ewan said before going silent. He discussed something with the soldiers of the Nation of the Spirit King who were also around. Once they walked away, Ewan approached Ruri.

"Something the matter?" Ruri questioned.

"I asked them to let you have lunch outside since you'll be out there anyway."

"Oh, wow! You're always making such thoughtful decisions, Ewan!"

"Heh heh, of course I am," Ewan said proudly, his head held high.

Ruri took Kotaro, Rin, the smaller spirits, and Ewan to the courtyard. The courtyard was left in a natural state, but it was well-maintained and not overgrown with weeds. It was an unrefined area with an emphasis on the peacefulness nature had to offer. It reminded Ruri in some ways of the area of forest where Chelsie lived.

They lay down in the shade of a large tree, and Ruri reclined against Kotaro. As they relaxed with Rin and the other spirits, several women walked up to her from the opposite direction. Ruri carried on without concern, but Ewan exercised caution. That was when she spotted Spinel, the girl from yesterday, among the pack of girls. She wanted to avoid talking to Spinel if she could, but since Spinel had no way of knowing that, she came straight toward Ruri.

She stopped in front of Ruri. Knowing that she couldn't remain lying down with Spinel right in front of her, Ruri sat up.

"Can I help you?" Ruri asked.

"I beg of you. Please separate from Master Jade," Spinel pleaded.

For a moment, Ruri had no idea what the girl was asking. She'd been wondering what Spinel had come to say with multiple women in tow, but she definitely hadn't expected Spinel to ask her to "separate from" her husband. Celestine would have been positively furious right about now. Ruri, on the other hand, was more exasperated than angry.

"No."

"Huh…?" Spinel looked surprised—which surprised Ruri.

"I mean, there isn't a fool alive who would separate from their spouse just because someone asked them nicely," Ruri explained.

Ewan and the spirits all nodded in agreement. Ruri looked at their reaction and felt relieved that she wasn't going insane.

Spinel's eyes started to water as she clenched both of her hands and scrunched her small and slender shoulders together. This weak and innocent display would have triggered a man's instinct to coddle and protect. That wasn't going to work on Ruri, though. And it wasn't going to work on Ewan, much less the spirits. They all gave her an icy glare.

Meanwhile, Spinel's entourage circled her as if to protect her. This just made it look like *Ruri* was the one bullying her.

"Master Jade said that he would come to pick me up. You being Master Jade's spouse is some kind of misunderstanding. I request that you return Master Jade to me."

This remark tested even Ruri's patience. "Jade-sama is *not* a thing. Return what to you? When did he become your property?"

"That…is not what I meant by…" Spinel trailed off, bursting into tears.

The girls around her immediately offered comforting words.

"Are you all right, Lady Spinel?"

"How utterly cruel."

"Can't you consider Lady Spinel's feelings?"

"There, there. Please do not cry, Lady Spinel."

Ruri looked on, boggled by the farce they were putting on.

Ewan turned around and met eyes with Ruri. Then they both nodded. Their minds were made up. They were going to run for it. Almost as if she were telepathically linked with Ewan, Ruri shot to her feet and slowly tried to move away. However, the girls quickly found her out.

"Wait a second, where might *you* be going?!"

"You're trying to leave after making Lady Spinel cry? How cold-blooded!"

Ruri stopped in her tracks, perplexed. The Nation of the Spirit King's people were supposed to be devoutly spirit-religious. Although it was slightly different here from the Nation of the Beast King, where they worshipped spirits, their treatment of those beloved by the spirits was appropriately polite. Even within the confines of the castle, they treated her better than Jade, the ruler of a whole nation. Despite that, Ruri felt no respect or esteem for Beloveds coming from the group of women.

Before she could figure out why that was, Ewan snapped at them first. "What do all of you think you're doing? This person is our nation's Beloved. Do you know just how rude you're being to a Beloved right now?!"

Ruri thought that Ewan, of all people, shouldn't be saying that, but she kept it to herself. Ewan had been extremely rude to Ruri at first due to his severe brother complex. Because of that, he wasn't the least bit convincing, but seeing how none of these women would know that, Ruri remained silent. She did know how to take a hint.

The girls shuddered for a second before quickly firing back.

"And so what if she is a Beloved?!"

"Lady Spinel is the distinguished daughter of the head nobles!"

A Beloved was a far bigger deal than the noblemen of a single nation, no matter how you sliced it. But these girls were speaking as if Spinel had more pull instead.

"And who cares?!" Ewan yelled. "Don't think that insolence toward a Beloved will be allowed just because you're from some head noble family! The Spirit King will be hearing about this! You better be prepared for an appropriate punishment!"

"Punishment!" the girls clamored, showing real fear as they turned to Spinel for help.

Spinel walked up to the front and said, "Please stop picking on these women. Are you saying that a Beloved is *that* important?!"

Ewan looked at her, mouth agape. Ruri was also taken aback, but she had a resistance to people like this. And it was all thanks to Asahi. Because Ruri knew Asahi, a person who would repeatedly make the most incoherent and dunderheaded claims, Ruri was quick to come back to her senses.

"If you're asking if they're important, then yes, they are," Ruri stated. "Important enough to make the king of a nation kneel before them, in fact. So what explains your attitudes? Are any of you truly citizens of this nation if you dare to throw mud in the face of the Spirit King? Even the people working in the markets know more about Beloveds than any of you."

"We are nobles. Lumping us in with the commoners working in the city is insolence itself!" replied Spinel.

Ruri was at a loss for words. But she also realized something.

"Uh, Ewan, we might have a problem…"

"Huh? What problem?"

Ruri peeked over at Kotaro and Rin. Ewan, intrigued, followed her line of sight until he reached the two supreme-level spirits, who both looked absolutely livid. Still, Ewan could only see Kotaro and Rin because they had physical bodies. The spirits around them that Ewan couldn't see were in battle mode, ready to pounce at the group of women at any moment.

"We gonna get 'em?"

"Let's get 'em."

"We should get 'em!"

"We should! We should!"

Ewan couldn't hear what they were saying, but he had a good hunch from the expression on Ruri's face.

"Is it bad? Is it *bad*?"

"It's terrible…"

More spirits were gathering from out of nowhere even now as the two of them panicked. And none of the women in front of them were any the wiser. Ruri finally realized that none of the women could see them.

"A 'Beloved' is nothing more than a sham anyway!" Spinel declared. "I've never seen any 'spirit.' You rely on that to act like you're someone important? Why, you're simply blackmailing Master Jade with that, aren't you?!"

"Hey, shut your trap!" Ewan angrily snapped, trying to keep her from inciting any more trouble with the spirits.

However, in Spinel's eyes, it looked as though her statement hit the nail right on the head. "Aah, I see from how flustered you are that there really *aren't* such things as Beloveds. Poor Master Jade. To think he would be so deceived."

Even more spirits gathered until the number was well out of hand.

"Punish anyone who picks on Ruri!"

"Bring down the hammer on anyone who speaks bad of Ruri!"

"Take down anyone who calls Ruri a liar!"

"Whoa! No, don't, don't!"

Just as Ruri was trying to contain the massive group of irritable spirits, a godsend arrived.

"What are you doing over there?" asked Lapis, the Beloved of the Nation of the Spirit King. "I was wondering what happened to get the spirits so upset…" He glared at Spinel with his father's patented stare.

"This girl was pickin' on Ruri!"

"She said that spirits don't exist!"

"She said that Beloveds are liars!"

Lapis once again glared at Spinel, having gotten the gist from the spirits' comments.

"Regardless of what you may think, disrespect toward another nation's Beloved is *not* allowed. I'll explain it in easier terms for you pack of morons to understand. She is the *Dragon Queen*. Any insolence you show her, the first wife of the Dragon King, is considered an act of treason against the Nation of the Dragon King. If you don't want to be arrested for disrespecting royalty, then disperse at once!"

Spinel grunted, her face twisting in frustration, but she gave Lapis a quick bow and walked off.

Ruri breathed a sigh of relief.

"I'm sorry for my countrymen's actions," Lapis apologized.

"Oh, don't worry. Thank you for coming to the rescue. If you hadn't come, then…" Ruri trailed off, looking over at the sea of still displeased-looking spirits. They'd been one step away from total disaster. She flashed him an awkward smile. "So hey, by any chance, can none of those girls see the spirits?"

"No, most likely not. The Nation of the Spirit King is similar to the Nation of the Dragon King in that the ratio of humans and demi-humans is about fifty-fifty. That group that just left was human. Since they have no mana, they can't see the spirits."

"But the Nation of the Spirit King's people believe in both spirits and Beloveds, so how did they turn out like that?"

"Because the Nation of the Spirit King is not monolithic. Most of them believe in spirits, and worship and adore them. That is why they all treat me, a Beloved, like family. But there are also those with little faith in the spirits, who doubt what they can't see. The families of those girls and Spinel's family fall in that category. Since their parents don't believe in them, neither do they."

"Huh? But isn't that problematic? Her parents are the head nobles, aren't they? The person who leads the nobles of the nation not believing in spirits or Beloveds?"

"No. With the House of Morga, the head of the house poses no problem. Neither does his first wife nor their children. However, Spinel's mother, the second wife, is a human from a foreign nation and does not believe in 'invisible' spirits. Spinel was raised and coddled by that mother of hers, so Spinel took after her and also insists that spirits don't exist. Not only that, but she was raised to get whatever she wanted as well, so she is the type to genuinely think that the world revolves around her. The fact that she thinks that way with no ill will makes it even worse."

"Ah, I see," Ruri said. She now understood why Spinel would ask her to break up with Jade; Spinel had a history of always getting what she wanted.

"That aside, you sure do know a lot, Lapis," Ruri noted.

"Well, yeah, I'm a Beloved," Lapis replied. "I can get any information if I feel so inclined. As for Spinel, her mother has been very persistent about making her daughter my first wife, so I'm pretty in the know because I did some digging on who they were."

"If she's looking to make her daughter your wife, then she must be one ambitious mother."

Lapis nodded. "I wouldn't doubt it if you told me that this whole 'the Dragon King coming to pick her up' story was the second wife essentially brainwashing her child into believing it to be true."

It seemed that the Nation of the Spirit King had its own set of problems.

After having lunch with Lapis, Ruri told Awain about what had happened. He bowed in apology, but she informed him that everything was all right because Lapis had helped her out. Still, the Spirit King decided that letting Spinel go unpunished wouldn't suffice, so he would deliver her punishment.

In the meantime, he sent notice to the head of the House of Morga that Spinel was not to attend the welcome party. Thanks to that, the party calmly proceeded, and a fun time was had by all.

The Case of the Sacred Beast Kidnapping

12

Ruri had taken Kotaro, Rin, and the other spirits to the forest at the back of the castle where the sacred beasts lived. No bodyguards accompanied them. The forest was sacred ground and off-limits to anyone but a select group of individuals. However, Ruri had said that she wanted to thank the sacred beasts for letting Kotaro have one of their kin's bodies, and since Awain couldn't refuse a Beloved's request, he'd given her permission to do so.

She should have actually visited them when she came to the Nation of the Spirit King on her honeymoon, but it had completely slipped her mind, and she had only remembered it once she was already on her way back home. She made it a point to go see the sacred beasts the next time she visited the nation.

After Awain granted her entry into the forest, Ruri had grabbed Kotaro and the others and happily headed there. Jade had been reluctant to let her go without security detail, but she'd pushed through anyway, saying that Kotaro and Rin would protect her instead. Jade had nothing to refute back with since she had the greatest form of security around—supreme-level spirits—so he very reluctantly saw her off.

Ruri entered the forest in high spirits. It was a regular fluffy, cuddly paradise.

"There are so many big Kotaros here," Ruri commented.

There were versions of Kotaro everywhere, all of them one or two sizes bigger than him. Some were resting underneath trees, tussling with each other in packs. It was a cuddly wuddly paradise. Ruri thought that maybe she should've brought Jade after all, but Jade liked smaller animals like cats and wasn't all that smitten with bigger creatures, even if they were just as soft and fluffy as Kotaro. She thought it was such a shame since she herself welcomed any and all cuddly creatures, regardless of size.

Suppressing her urge to glomp the furry beasts, Ruri slowly approached them. According to Awain, the sacred beasts were highly intelligent and fully capable of understanding human speech. These were not your run-of-the-mill animals, which was why, rather than treat them as such, Ruri decided to give them proper courtesy as equal beings.

"Very nice to meet you. My name is Ruri!" she greeted with a bow.

The sacred beasts in the vicinity turned toward Ruri and gathered around her in droves. She'd heard that they were docile creatures, but the overwhelming pressure they exuded almost made her fall back. Thankfully, she managed to get a grip on herself.

Among the sacred beasts that had huddled over to her, a very big one sat in front of Ruri and pushed its nose against her hand. It sniffed her scent a few times before it suddenly looked up at the sky and howled. The other sacred beasts followed suit and howled as well.

"Huh? *Huh*?" Ruri asked, puzzled.

Kotaro came to her side and explained, "*He says Ruri is welcome among them.*"

Relieved to know that she hadn't done anything wrong, Ruri thanked the sacred beasts once they were finished with their cries. "Thank you very much for giving that body to Kotaro. I know he was still just a pup... But rest assured, Kotaro will take good care of him."

The biggest sacred beast stared into Ruri's eyes. Then it nuzzled its nose against hers. Ruri responded to the rather sweet gesture by timidly patting its head. Its fur was just a little coarser than Kotaro's, and it had enough of it to engulf her entire hand.

"It's so soft and fluffy…" Ruri said, her expression naturally softening.

"*It seems that they've accepted Ruri,*" Rin chimed in.

"Y-Yes, indeed…" Kotaro stammered, somewhat bothered that Ruri was enjoying petting anyone other than himself. Ruri hadn't noticed it, but Rin did, and she gave a small chuckle.

The sacred beasts then took turns giving Ruri a nose nuzzle greeting. Ruri petted each head that was presented to her and, in the process, noticed something.

"Everyone here is bigger than Kotaro, and I don't see any smaller pups."

"*No, there is a pup that was recently born here, but they're off playing somewhere else in the forest,*" Kotaro noted.

"Is it safe to leave a baby alone?" Ruri wondered.

"*Newborn as they may be, they are still a wild animal. They don't need adults to hold their hands when they walk, like human children do. Also, there are no natural predators who prey on sacred beasts in this forest. They should face no danger even if they wander freely around. It also looks like Trees is keeping an eye on the area as well. That wasn't the case the last time I came here, so it seems something happened.*"

"Something like?"

"*Remember, my body is that of a child. And yet that child died… here, in a forest where no natural predators dwell. Some sort of problem must have arisen in that area. That has nothing to do with me, though.*"

"Well, technically, yes, but…" Ruri mumbled. She sometimes found it hard to keep up with the spirits' dry behavior. They would try to protect her to the point of excess, but then they'd show disinterest to the point of being cold-blooded toward others. But that was how spirits operated, and the only ones who held their interest were Beloveds. In that sense, being a Beloved was like being born with a very unique feature.

It wasn't unreasonable that the nobles of the Imperial Nation wanted a Beloved, but Ruri fortunately never came across any of them. That was apparently because Finn and Claus had worked behind the scenes to keep it that way. Ruri spent her short time in the forest thinking that she should thank them when everything was over.

The next morning, after breakfast, Ruri strolled around the castle with Jade and the spirits. Not long after they began, they noticed that the soldiers were running to and fro, causing a commotion.

"I wonder what's going on?" Ruri asked.

"Maybe something happened?" Jade speculated.

The two of them curiously walked along until they found Awain and Lapis. Awain was barking orders at his soldiers.

"Search outside the castle walls just in case! And search every corner of the forest again! They might be in a hole somewhere! Lapis, what about your end?"

"I'm having them search right now, but they still haven't found anything."

Awain and Lapis wore grim expressions that looked so similar when they stood side by side that it made it abundantly clear that the two were father and son. Be that as it may, it seemed that a problem had arisen.

Ruri went with Jade to address Awain. The soldiers realized Jade was there and opened a path for him.

"Awain, is there a problem?" Jade asked.

"Oh, it's you, Jade. Well, a *small* problem, yes…" Awain said in an intentionally vague manner. He noticed Kotaro standing next to Ruri and stared straight at him. Then Awain knelt in front of Kotaro and asked, "O Lord Spirit of Wind, could you please lend me a helping hand?"

"*I have no reason to lend you any help,*" Kotaro curtly refused.

Awain looked disappointed, but he didn't say anything more. He most likely knew that it would be a waste of time to try to convince a spirit to do something they had no interest in. Ruri, on the other hand, couldn't just pretend not to care after seeing how stressed Awain was.

"Spirit King, what happened? Is it something Kotaro could help with?"

Awain looked indecisive. He looked at Ruri, then at Kotaro, and slowly started explaining.

"The thing is, we've lost sight of a sacred beast cub. And that's causing an uproar from the sacred beasts."

"Wha?! That's terrible news, then! Oh, is that why you want Kotaro to search?"

"Indeed."

Ruri looked at Kotaro. "Kotaro?" she said with a pleading look in her eyes. She gave him that look because she knew he would help if it was her asking, but Kotaro didn't agree right away.

"*What about Trees? I felt the presence of his power over there. Trees could find out where they are without having to go through the trouble of asking me, could he not?*"

"Well, it seems that not even the Spirit of Trees knows where they are," Awain stated.

"*What? Really?*" Kotaro replied, sounding surprised.

Just then, a voice descended from out of nowhere. "*Wind, I'm asking you personally. Find the sacred beast child.*"

"Oh, it's the Spirit of Trees!" cried voices from all around.

"*You're not able to track them down?*" Kotaro asked.

"*I am not. Sacred beasts never leave the forest. Essentially, though I don't know how they did it, it seems that someone slipped past my eyes and kidnapped the pup.*"

"*But it's nigh impossible for anyone to slip past your eyes, Trees,*" Kotaro noted.

"*Yes, I am aware, but the sacred beast is no longer in the forest. I need the power of wind to search for them.*"

"*I suppose I'll do it, then…*" Kotaro agreed with a sigh.

"*It's appreciated,*" the Spirit of Trees said before his voice faded away.

Kotaro then summoned wind around him and dispersed it across the area.

"*The range is wide. It will take a while.*"

"Many thanks," Awain replied, giving Kotaro his nation's highest form of salute.

"Anyway, when did the pup go missing?" Ruri asked, unable to contribute since she hadn't seen any pups when she went to the forest yesterday.

"It seems they noticed this morning," Awain explained with a weary sigh. "The sacred beasts let the child run free because they figured that the forest was safe, but the pup didn't show up when the caretakers went to feed them this morning. We've had the Spirit of Trees search the area, but it turns out that they cannot find them." Awain went on to explain that the other sacred beasts, with their strong camaraderie, had been in an uproar and that pacifying them had been a huge struggle.

That was when they all heard it.

"I saw the Beloved of the Nation of the Dragon King go into the forest yesterday."

The intruding voice belonged to Spinel, who had been present for an indeterminate amount of time, listening in on the conversation.

"The forest is off-limits to but a handful of people. In which case, the Beloved would be the only one with a chance to abduct the pup, would she not?" Spinel said, shaking the crowd. "After all, the only outsider who entered the forest was the Nation of the Dragon King's Beloved. Plus, she already has a sacred beast serving by her side. Is it not likely that she wanted another one?"

"I didn't see the sacred beast pup when I visited the forest yesterday," Ruri hastily refuted, afraid that at this rate she might be misconstrued as the culprit.

"Those words mean nothing. You did not take any bodyguards with you into the forest, did you? No one else was watching you."

"I had the spirits with me."

"Spirits? Something you can't even *see* is no witness."

"That's only because *you* can't see them. They were right by my side the entire time," Ruri insisted, gradually getting more annoyed at Spinel and her spirit-denying attitude.

"Spirits don't—"

"That is *enough*!" Awain shouted, cutting off Spinel before she had a chance to argue anymore. If he'd let her continue, she would have uttered something that would've been completely irreversible.

Oblivious to the fact that Awain had actually helped her, Spinel furrowed her brow.

At first, Ruri had thought that Spinel was a well-mannered aristocrat's daughter, but she was actually a walking landmine.

Kotaro and the other spirits were on the verge of exploding at Spinel, who was denying their existence and treating Ruri like the culprit. However, Spinel was the only one in the room who didn't see any of this. The soldiers around her all went deathly pale.

"You need to watch your tongue, Spinel. She is not only a Beloved, but the Dragon Queen of the Nation of the Dragon King," Awain warned her.

Kotaro, a spirit with a physical body, should have been visible to Spinel. Did that not register with her? And didn't she realize that denying spirits existed, right in front of a fully visible spirit named Kotaro, was a very problematic action for the head noble's daughter in the Nation of the Spirit King? Judging from Spinel's attitude, she probably didn't comprehend that. She didn't appear to understand what she'd done wrong for the Spirit King to scold her.

"I wish to ask the spirits something," Awain declared. "Did Ruri kidnap the sacred beast pup?"

"*That is impossible,*" Kotaro answered.

Rin nodded. "*Yes, there is no way. We can testify.*"

After the two supreme-level spirits gave their word, the other lesser spirits unanimously testified as well.

"*Ruri didn't do anything like that!*"

"*That's right! That's right!*"

"*Ruri didn't do anything bad!*"

"And there you have it. The rest of you should not be misled by such foolish statements," Awain said after going through the hassle of asking Kotaro and Rin to testify on Ruri's behalf.

Spirits did not lie, not even for a Beloved. Everyone other than Spinel knew this to be so and, satisfied with the answer, decided to go about their business. Spinel then disappeared, mingling into the dispersing crowd.

After that, Ruri had to deal with another problem.

"*She is such a jerk~!*"

"*Should we put her out of commission?*"

"*Let's make it so she never comes near Ruri ever again~!*"

"No, no! Absolutely not!"

"*Aww~!*" the spirits cried with disappointment in unison, almost as if they were asking why she was stopping them.

Ruri was about to ask Kotaro and Rin for assistance, but…

"*Ruri, let's get her,*" Kotaro suggested.

"*Fully agree. Let's crush that wench,*" Rin demanded.

Both spirits were absolutely serious. Ruri could do nothing but slump in response.

"My apologies," Awain interjected, "but she is one of my nation's own. I would like to deal with her, if possible." He knew he was dealing with two supreme-level spirits, so he requested this with modesty so as to avoid the worst-case scenario.

"*But that wench is annoying,*" Rin retorted, circling around Kotaro.

"*Agreed,*" Kotaro added.

Rin began to vent, saying, "*It's whatever that she doesn't believe in spirits, but to use that as a reason to pick a fight with Ruri? Is she an idiot? There is a Beloved in this very nation, for crying out loud. Was she given any semblance of a proper education?*"

"I have no words to offer," Awain replied apologetically. But according to Lapis, the way in which the House of Morga had educated her was to blame. "I will give the House of Morga another warning."

"*I can't imagine that fixing things, though,*" Rin grumbled. "*Oh well. I'd rather Ruri not be accused of being the culprit again, so I'll pitch in to help search for the real perpetrator too.*"

"I'll help!"

"Let's do it!"

"Oh yeah!"

Jade looked at the clamoring spirits with extreme dread. "Ruri, you're going to have to act as the stopper here."

"Well, I'm not too sure that I *can* stop them, but I will try," Ruri replied.

Afraid that the spirits would go berserk and bring disaster to the Nation of the Spirit King, Ruri reluctantly decided to take part in the investigation.

The Criminal Treatment

Ruri and the spirits had started their search for the missing pup, but several days had passed, and they'd found neither hide nor hair of it. Kotaro couldn't hide his frustration and slapped his tail harshly across the floor. Rin was also at her wit's end.

"If Kotaro can't find them, they're either using Spirit Slayer or the Spirit of Light's power," Rin proposed.

"The Spirit of Light?" Ruri asked.

"The Spirit of Light's barriers are stronger than any other spirit's. It has the power to isolate those within its boundaries from the outside world. And if they felt so inclined, they could also kidnap a sacred beast under the nose of Trees, like with our current case..."

"But the Spirit of Light is back at the Nation of the Dragon King's castle, isn't she?" Ruri asked, positive that she'd seen the supreme-level spirit back at the harbor waving goodbye.

"Indeed," Kotaro confirmed. *"Light had crossed my mind as well, so I checked, but she's back at the Nation of the Dragon King as we left her. She said that she didn't know anything about what happened to the sacred beast."*

Spirits had their own unique way of communicating, so they could contact one another even if they were far away—a very handy power to have for times like this.

"Then…you don't think that whoever did it is using Spirit Slayer, do you?"

They had made Yadacain, a nation of witches, stop using Spirit Slayer magic, and the Spirit of Darkness was there keeping tabs to ensure that no one tried. Still, if it *wasn't* Spirit Slayer…

"*No, it's not,*" Rin asserted. "*Trees has been keeping an eye on that forest for some time now. There's no way that he wouldn't have noticed Spirit Slayer in use.*"

"Hmm, that raises even *more* questions, then," Ruri pondered.

"*I am at a loss myself,*" Kotaro replied.

"Well, like they say, seeing is believing, and you never leave any stone unturned at the scene of the crime. Want to go to the forest and actually see if we can find anything?"

"*I suppose it's better than sitting around here,*" Kotaro commented.

"*Yes, let's check it out,*" Rin agreed.

Ruri then went to Awain to ask for permission. Fearing that something else might happen or that Ruri might be blamed for something she didn't do again, Awain sent Lapis and some of the Nation of the Spirit King's soldiers to accompany her for this venture.

Once they reached the forest, Ruri noticed that the relaxed atmosphere from last time was gone. The sacred beasts were seething with rage. The nation was going to have a different set of problems on its hands if they didn't find that pup soon.

"A child of the sacred beasts was killed in the past," Lapis explained. "While we don't know whether this pup is alive, this marks the second time that their young has been taken from them."

The child that had been killed was the original owner of the body Kotaro was currently using. Admittedly, Kotaro had been *given* the deceased body, but the point stood.

"The pup that owned Kotaro's body was killed?" Ruri asked in surprise, unaware of that fact.

"Yeah, its caretaker at the time poisoned its food. The unsuspecting child consumed it and died. The perpetrator has already been apprehended, but there are a lot of points that raise suspicions."

"Like what?"

"Don't know. My father is in charge of the nation's affairs. It's not good for a Beloved to know too much."

"Didn't you brag about how you could get any info you wanted if you felt so inclined before?"

"That's one matter, and this is another." In other words, Lapis wasn't really interested. "My dad is working on those issues as we speak, so don't worry about it."

"But if there was an issue involving the sacred beasts in the past, there might be some sort of connection," Ruri suggested.

"I'm sure my dad is looking into that as well. What you can do right now is search for the pup, Ruri. You'll naturally learn who the culprit is that way as well, right?"

"Grk, it's frustrating to hear *you* make a sound argument…"

Lapis was a problematic character who fell in love at first sight at the drop of a hat, but he was right about this. The spirits were so cross at the fact that Ruri was being labeled a criminal that she had no choice but to accompany them on the search. Normally, however, since Ruri was another nation's Beloved, she wouldn't be at liberty to stick her nose into this nation's affairs.

After seeing that the eager spirits had spread out through the forest, Ruri had nothing much else to do, so she patiently waited. Sadly, even after several hours of searching, they were unable to find anything. The group had no choice but to return to the castle empty handed.

As soon as Ruri stepped through the doors, Celestine stormed up to her. "What is the meaning of this, Lady Ruri?!"

Ruri wanted to ask the same question since the first thing that came out of Celestine's mouth was an angry tirade.

"The meaning of what, per se?" Ruri ventured.

"'Meaning of what,' indeed! The whole castle is ablaze with rumors of you killing the sacred beast pup."

"Pardon?!" Ruri asked. She was so shocked that her eyes nearly popped out of her head. "Where did *that* rumor come from?!"

"That is what *I* would like to hear. My caretaker told me that word is quickly spreading through the castle. Are you sticking your neck into danger again? You *always* seem to have issues hanging around you."

"I mean, it's not my fault that tends to happen..." Ruri muttered.

"At any rate, come this way, please," Celestine said, grabbing Ruri's arm and dragging Ruri with her.

Before she could even ask where Celestine was taking her, she found herself in a room with the top brass of the four nations already assembled.

"Oh, everyone is here. Did I come at a good time?" asked Ruri.

"Yes, we were just talking about you," Jade replied.

"About me?" she asked, taking the seat next to Jade as Celestine took the one on Jade's other side—a seating arrangement that seemed almost set in stone at this point.

Once Lapis also sat down, everyone started discussing the rumors that Celestine had mentioned earlier.

"Apparently, some rather unsavory rumors about you are spreading, Ruri," Jade told her.

"Yes, it sure seems so," Ruri remarked in a carefree tone.

Jade smiled wryly. "Ruri, you ought to show a little concern."

"Why? They're just rumors, aren't they?" Ruri asked, confident that the spirits would refute any claim that she'd committed the crime.

Jade, however, saw danger imminent. "Never underestimate the power rumors hold. You never know when they might pull the rug out from under you. And that could result in…" Jade trailed off, peeking at Kotaro and Rin.

Ruri glanced that way as well and understood what he meant. *She* wouldn't be the one exploding with anger if anything happened to a Beloved. It would be the spirits.

"So, where are these rumors coming from?" Ruri asked.

"We're currently investigating that," Awain answered, pressing his temples. "The rumors seem to be circulating around the nobles who can't see spirits—a handful of those who aren't dedicated to worshipping spirits or Beloveds, you see. It's headache-inducing, but some only pay their respects to Lapis because he is my son. They doubt his status as a Beloved. That very handful of people who can't see spirits are the ones buying into the rumors."

There were rumors spreading everywhere about Ruri, a woman who was not only another nation's Beloved, but the contract-bearer to several supreme-level spirits. Along with the sacred beast's disappearance, Awain's stomach was in trouble. Stomach medicine was certainly in his future.

"Those who can see spirits know very well how fearsome they can be," Jade said.

Everyone present nodded in agreement. Accusing a Beloved without any proof was essentially picking a fight with the spirits themselves.

"Ruri, we're currently investigating the source of the rumors. We're also working toward quashing them. So, please, if you can…" Awain started.

"Yes, I'll be fine, so please don't worry," Ruri replied, finishing Awain's sentence and assuring him that she would be all right.

Relief washed over Awain's face. Ruri didn't want to exacerbate his worries any more, but then Kotaro interrupted.

"*Ruri.*"

"What is it, Kotaro?"

"*Can we exterminate that bratty girl after all?*"

"Wait, who are you talking about?!" Ruri asked.

"*The same brat that's been trying to accuse you of things you haven't done.*"

"Oh, are you talking about that 'Spinel' girl?"

"*Indeed, I am. It looks like she is the source of the rumors. She is even making disparaging remarks about you in the castle as we speak. Saying that you killed the sacred beast.*"

"Aww, come on. She *is*?"

Unlike Ruri, who simply looked annoyed, Awain looked as if he saw a ghost. "That *idiot*! Someone! Is someone out there?!" Awain screamed toward the corridor.

A soldier standing at attention outside quickly entered. "You called, sire?"

"Bring me Spinel, wherever she is in the castle, *this instant*. And bring me the head of the House of Morga. He should be in the castle as well!"

"Yes! At once, sire!"

As soon as the soldier left the room, the Spirit King clutched his head, ready to pull his hair out—literally. The other three rulers looked at him sympathetically.

After a while, Spinel was brought into the room along with a plump middle-aged man who had a tiny mustache. This man was the head of the House of Morga. He was sweating and panting, probably because he'd run here. Spinel, on the other hand, looked cool and composed, performing an exquisite bow in front of all of the leaders.

145

Though Spinel seemed to be well-raised and properly educated on the surface, her ignorance became apparent once the spirits were involved. She had most likely been instilled with some very biased ideologies. Then again, perhaps it was inevitable that she wouldn't believe in the spirits since she couldn't see them. But it made her ill-equipped to be the head noble's daughter in the Nation of the *Spirit* King—a nation that housed a Beloved.

There was a huge difference between the head of the House of Morga and his daughter. He cowered under the sharp gaze of the leaders in attendance, whereas Spinel stood looking at Jade with flushed cheeks.

"Morga," called Awain.

"Sire!" the head of the House of Morga answered back.

"You are aware of the rumors circulating through the castle about the Nation of the Dragon King's Beloved, correct?"

"I am. As the head noble, I am appalled that such rumors debasing the Lady Beloved are being spread in the castle of the Nation of the Spirit King."

"Do you believe those words to be enough when you hear that your *daughter* is the source of said rumors?"

"I beg your pardon?!" he exclaimed in surprise, staring at his daughter. "Spinel, is this true?!"

"Whatever are you talking about?" Spinel hummed, blatantly playing dumb.

Awain shot her an icy look and declared, "The supreme-level Spirit of Wind has seen and heard everything. You will *not* talk your way out of this."

Spinel then furrowed her brow. "With all due respect, Your Majesty, a spirit's word is not trustworthy. Spirits are mere idols. They do not actually exist."

"You heard the girl, Morga. What are you teaching this daughter of yours? She not only lives in the Nation of the Spirit King, but she is the daughter of a head noble. Yet here she is delivering this nonsense."

"A-A thousand apologies! Her mother is from a foreign land and lacks mana of her own. Spinel believes not in spirits and has been greatly influenced by her mother's ways. By the time I took notice and tried to reeducate her, her stereotypes were already too deeply ingrained, and there was no convincing her. That is why I am in the midst of arranging for her to be wed in another nation that isn't as spirit-religious, as I suspect it would be hard for her to continue living here in the Nation of the Spirit King."

"I see. You do have a point. She is so entrenched in her ways that it's doubtful she'd change. So, *when* are you going to marry her off?" Awain asked with a tone that was practically demanding that he do it now.

"Sire! Just as soon as preparations are set!"

"Wait just a second! Send me off to be *married*? What do you mean?!" Spinel asked, evidently not privy to this plan.

"Do you know how much trouble you've caused the Lady Beloved in the past few days? I can't allow someone with such dangerous ideologies to remain as the daughter of this nation's head nobles. The least I can do as your father is find you a good family to marry into. If you are opposed to that, then you will have to live on your own as a commoner."

"B-But I'm going to be Master Jade's wife!"

Ruri met eyes with Jade and smiled awkwardly, realizing that Spinel still was not over that matter.

"Dragonkin can only love one spouse. His Majesty the Dragon King is already married. You *can't* be His Majesty's wife," the head noble replied.

"I don't know anything about that. Also, I was told that I would be Master Jade's wife when I became of age," Spinel proclaimed.

"Who in blazes told you something so preposterous? His Majesty made no such promise to you," the head argued.

"It was mother. Mother told me that Master Jade would one day come to take my hand in marriage!"

As the father and daughter continued to argue, the true circumstances behind Jade's supposed cheating finally came to light. The head of the House of Morga was also starting to develop a headache.

"That…imbecile…" the head noble hissed as he became yet another person who needed stomach medicine to cure what ailed him.

"I see. So your mother said that I would come to get you when you were of age, then?" Jade asked.

"Yes, indeed she did!" Spinel happily replied.

"Oh, I see," Ruri remarked. "Well, I'm glad to know that you didn't try to put your hands on a child, Jade-sama. Otherwise, people would have continued to suspect you were some sort of pedophile."

"Ruri…" Jade groaned, sullenly staring at her. She turned her head in response.

Spinel's mother was also trying to get her daughter hitched to Lapis, so she likely was an extremely power-hungry individual. Ruri wanted to ask Spinel's mother if she thought she had any shot of marrying her daughter off to Jade after making her think that spirits weren't real. Spinel seemed the type to have some pretty *radical* preconceptions, so maybe the apple didn't fall far from the tree. Spinel's mother definitely wasn't a woman you'd want to get heavily involved with.

"I'll leave you to deal with those matters, Morga," Awain concluded.

"Very well, sire. I will begin preparations for my daughter's wedding at once."

"Father?!" Spinel exclaimed in a criticizing tone.

Nevertheless, the head of the House of Morga gave it no mind and continued, "I will have these rumors extinguished immediately as well."

"Please do so. You may go now."

"I offer my humble apologies for any inconvenience she may have caused all of you," the head of the House of Morga said before leaving the room, dragging Spinel with him. Spinel was saying something to Jade as her father carted her out, but no one paid it any attention.

Once the two of them were completely out of the room, everyone left heaved a sigh.

"It seems that even a kingdom as old as the Nation of the Spirit King has its fair share of headaches," noted the emperor of the Imperial Nation, Adularia. She was sympathetic as she herself had to deal with troublesome nobles.

Awain could do nothing but agree and nod his head. "You can say that again. It's times like these when I just feel like giving up the throne." Awain had been king of his nation since its inception, which meant the weight on his shoulders was in a different league.

"Anyway, I think it's fair to say this case is closed," Arman finished.

"Yes, she probably won't be bothering you anymore if she is being married off to another nation," Celestine added.

Ruri listened to Arman's and Celestine's quips with some confusion. "Is it common for parents to decide on their children's marriages in this world?"

"Depends on the nation, race, and other factors," Jade explained. "Some marriages are born out of love like you and me, while others are politically driven to strengthen the ties between families. The latter is especially common among nobles in the Imperial Nation and the Nation of the Spirit King."

"Oh wow. That means it's less common in the Nation of the Dragon King?"

"That it does. We have no aristocrats in the Nation of the Dragon King, and dragonkin themselves advocate for romantic marriages. That doesn't mean that other types of marriages don't exist at all, though. There are places where it's common for the family to decide on marriages, depending on the race of the family."

Ruri had felt awkward because she'd married out of mutual love, but after hearing Jade's elaboration, she thought it was actually pretty similar to how it worked in her world.

Just when everyone thought things were settled…

"Oh my, do you mean we can't punish that girl?" asked Rin.

"Grrr…" growled Kotaro.

"Aww~!"

"We can't give her just one punch?"

"Even just a li'l bit?"

All of the spirits started to grumble in discontent, but Awain somehow managed to smooth things over with them.

The Elixir

Ruri had thought that the rumors would die down, but they had spread further than anyone had expected. Walking around the castle was uncomfortable, to say the least.

"I can't believe she can strut around so calmly."

"Never thought there would be a Beloved wild enough to kill a sacred beast."

"Isn't His Majesty going to punish her?"

They might have been trying to keep their voices down, but Ruri could hear them perfectly fine. The majority of them sounded dubious, but there was an extremely small number of people who truly believed the rumors and were speaking ill of her. Since her reputation was directly linked to that of the Nation of the Dragon King, she needed to clear her good name as quickly as possible, and the best way to do that was to locate the sacred beast pup.

One night, Ruri stalked about the castle in cat form, figuring that she could gain intel she couldn't gain in human form. Walking around with the spirits in tow just put people on alert, and Kotaro's sacred beast body was notably conspicuous, so she'd brought only Rin along and left the other spirits behind in her room. Kotaro and the other spirits had opposed the idea at first, but with Kotaro's barrier around her at all times and Rin accompanying her, Ruri had managed to convince them.

As Ruri walked around, the wind would occasionally caress her body. It coiled around her as if protecting her, proof that Kotaro was watching over her from afar. Having him by her side without him actually being by her side was extremely reassuring.

Ruri wandered around, passing by the occasional soldier, until she started seeing fewer and fewer people. Just when she contemplated turning back because she'd gone a little too far out, a familiar individual crossed in front of her.

"*Huh? Spinel?*" Ruri murmured.

"*Seems so. I could never forget such an annoying face,*" replied Rin.

Ruri and Rin chased after her, curious as to what Spinel was up to this late at night. She was heading somewhere while keeping a careful eye on her surroundings.

"*Suspicious… That girl is definitely suspicious,*" Rin stated.

"*Isn't that just how it looks to you because you hate her, Rin?*" Ruri countered.

"*Okay, but don't you find it strange that a young girl like her is walking around at this hour?*"

"*Well, I can't really speak about others here. I'm in the same boat.*"

"*Uh, yes, which is why it's suspicious!*"

"*Rin, be quiet. She'll find us out,*" Ruri said with a gasp. Much to her relief, Spinel hadn't noticed either of them. "*Anyway, I wonder where she's going?*"

Spinel exited the building in secret, heading toward the gardens. In the dark of night, Ruri followed her and walked through the barely visible garden until she saw a small shed-like building, one that the gardeners used as a storehouse.

Going toward the back of the shed, Spinel suddenly stopped and asked, "Are you here?"

Ruri heard a rustling sound and figured someone else was there, but she couldn't see who it was from where she stood. Still, she hesitated to get any closer for fear Spinel would spot them.

"*Rin, ask Kotaro to make out the face of the person she's talking to.*"

"*Got it,*" Rin replied.

It wasn't long before Ruri felt the wind wafting around her, perhaps spurred by Rin.

"If you're here, then come out immediately!" Spinel demanded.

"Sorry. I'm struggling to keep *myself* hidden, you see," said the person talking to Spinel, who, judging from the voice, was male. His voice didn't sound very old either, so it belonged to a young man.

"In any case, I ask that you show yourself," Spinel insisted. "It's hard to talk to someone I cannot see."

"Hey, I'm the cautious type. We can chat just like this, can't we?"

"Well, whatever. So where is the thing I requested?"

"I've got it nice and stashed away," the young man answered. "In a place no one'll find, that is."

"Where is it? Please hand it over."

"Whoa there, not yet. I need you to pay me if we're going to do business."

"I...do not have it right now."

"Then this deal is a bust. I'll return the sacred beast to the forest."

Ruri almost gasped hearing the words "sacred beast," but she kept it inside as best she could. She couldn't allow herself to be discovered right now.

"Wait! I will get your payment ready," Spinel asserted. "So give me the pup first. I need the elixir."

"You mean that elixir drawn from sacred beasts, eh? I never knew that you could extract an elixir like that from them, but I can't wrap my head around why you'd be willing to risk so much to get it."

"Even if you don't, I *need* it. I couldn't get the other sacred beast before, even though I convinced its caretaker to come to my side and had him poison it. If I let this chance slip by, then I will be at the end of my rope."

"Ha ha ha, you're one scary girl," the young man remarked. "Not even *I'm* crazy enough to want a girl like you in my life."

Spinel sniffed. "Your sentiment matters not to me. For I have Master Jade."

"Right, right. Knock yourself out with that. Anyway, just bring my payment. Then we can talk business. We'll meet again in three days' time. If you can't get my payment by then, the deal's off, and I return this little guy to the forest."

"Yes…very well."

Ruri and Rin waited until the two had left the area before finally moving.

"*This is terrible,*" Ruri said, rushing for dear life to Jade.

When she returned to their room, Jade was waiting for her with a furrowed brow. His face was a bit flushed because he'd been drinking with Awain and Arman, but he didn't appear to be too drunk. Once he returned to the room, he'd noticed that Ruri was missing, so it was only natural that he would be displeased.

Now was not the time for a lecture, however. After Ruri had Jade remove her bracelet and she reverted back to human form, she desperately tried to tell him the news.

"It's terrible, Jade-sama! We need to go to the Spirit King *right now*!"

"It's the dead of night. You should hold off until tomorrow. And besides, where were you off to at this hour in cat form? You shouldn't go out without securit—"

"I know who kidnapped the sacred beast!"

Jade's brows instantly shifted. "You do?"

"I do, which is why I need to speak with the Spirit King."

"Okay, then. I'll request a meeting," Jade replied and asked a soldier outside the room to contact Awain.

In the meantime, Ruri asked Kotaro, "Kotaro, did you see his face?"

After some silence, Kotaro shook his head.

"Huh? How come?"

"*I couldn't see it for some reason. My powers were rejected, as if they bounced off of something. I wasn't able to track him down either.*"

"*Wha? What do you mean?*" Rin pressed. She found Kotaro's answer unexpected as well.

"*I do not know myself. It might be related to why I'm unable to find the sacred beast. But it's almost like…*"

"'Almost like'?" Ruri prodded.

"*Well, it feels like when I bounced off of Light's power,*" Kotaro explained.

"But the Spirit of Light is in the Nation of the Dragon King and doesn't know anything, right?"

"*Indeed. She said so, and she was telling no lie.*"

This was begging more and more questions, but at least they knew that the kidnapper was a man and that some sort of power was in effect.

As they contemplated the peculiarities, they went to meet with the Spirit King. Ruri had thought only Awain would be in the room, but when they arrived, there sat Lapis. Awain prompted them to take a seat, and Ruri began speaking without a second's delay.

"I saw Spinel when I went walking around the castle just now."

"Ruri, this isn't the Nation of the Dragon King, so you can't act so rashly…" Jade chided.

"Oh, come on, Jade-sama. Please don't interrupt me while I'm speaking. Stay quiet, will you?" Ruri said, ignoring Jade as she continued to speak. "Anyway, she went to an unpopulated part of the gardens and met up with someone there."

"Who is this 'someone'?" asked Awain.

"Well, I couldn't see his face, but he was a young man going by his voice. I listened in on their conversation and the man said he kidnapped the sacred beast."

"What?!" Awain exclaimed, leaning forward.

"He said that he hid it somewhere, but he didn't mention where. He was there to carry out some sort of deal with Spinel, and Spinel had ordered him to kidnap the beast in the first place. However, the negotiations broke down because Spinel couldn't pay him. He said they would try again in three days, and if she can't pay him by then, he would return the pup to the forest."

"Essentially meaning that Spinel was the orchestrator," Awain surmised, placing his hand on his forehead. He was unable to hide his shock.

"Not only that, but Spinel is connected with the murder of the sacred beast from last time. She said she partnered with the caretaker and poisoned it."

"Why in the world would Spinel do such a thing?"

"She mentioned something about an elixir," Ruri added.

Jade looked confused, but Awain and Lapis looked completely flabbergasted.

"Spinel said that? About an elixir?" Awain questioned.

"Yes. Right, Rin?" Ruri asked, looking at Rin, who nodded in confirmation.

"This is unbelievable. How does Spinel know about the elixir?"

"Well, she *is* the daughter of the head noble, despite appearances," Lapis said, calmly admonishing his father. "Her family still holds pertinent documents, so there's a chance she learned it from those, right?"

"Erm... What is the elixir from sacred beasts?" Ruri asked.

Awain and Lapis quickly clammed up. They most likely didn't want to divulge the secret if at all possible. That didn't matter to the spirits, though.

"You can gather a special material from a sacred beast's corpse and use it as an ingredient for a medicine," Rin explained.

Awain and Lapis, who'd been hesitating, were stunned. Regardless, Rin didn't stop.

"This nation protected sacred beasts, which were on the brink of extinction because of this, from overhunting."

"What kind of medicine can you make from it?" Ruri asked.

"Ah, please wait!" Awain pleaded in a panic, but Rin didn't even give him a passing look.

"A medicine that controls people."

Awain covered his face as if saying, "Oh, brother."

"It allows you to bend whoever drinks it to your will."

"Wait, isn't that *really bad*?" Ruri asked.

"Of course it's bad. That's why the elixir is kept under wraps, and only a select handful of people in this nation know of it. So Awain is saying it's strange that Spinel would know of it in spite of that."

"Oh, I see now." Once Rin finished with her explanation, Ruri turned her attention from Rin to Awain. That was when she noticed the weird tension in the air. "Is there something the matter?"

"As Lady Spirit of Water detailed, the elixir is only known to a very small group of people. That's why I wanted to abstain from telling you, if possible..." Awain admitted as he looked at Rin bitterly.

"Oh my, it's fine. Ruri's lips aren't loose enough to blab secrets to others," Rin said in an aloof manner.

Awain slumped. "Ruri, Jade, this is a top secret issue, so please don't tell anyone else."

"R-Right," replied Jade.

"Yes, sire…" echoed Ruri.

Ruri and Jade, taking pity on Awain, responded earnestly as they resumed their conversation.

"So why would Spinel want that elixir?" Jade asked.

Rin snorted. *"Isn't it obvious? To make you drink it, king."*

All eyes turned to Jade, and a grimace formed on his lips.

Just then, Awain remembered something. "Come to think of it, you did come to the Nation of the Spirit King for a meeting after the last sacred beast was killed, didn't you, Jade? Perhaps that was when she was going to make you drink it."

Fortunately, Kotaro had gotten to the body before Spinel could.

"A very close call," Ruri remarked. "Jade-sama, you should thank Kotaro."

"Yes… You're right…" Jade uttered, looking very pale. Although, considering that he'd just heard that he might have been a target of this drug, it was only natural.

"Well, what do we do?" Ruri asked. "We may know that Spinel is the culprit, but not even Kotaro could track down the perpetrator, so we have no idea where the pup is."

"Not even Lord Spirit of Wind could track him down?" Awain said, surprised.

"Nope."

Awain and Jade both furrowed their brows. Although Jade still looked fine, Awain's tense visage made him look extremely scary. Ruri kept that to herself, however, and waited for the two men to gather their thoughts.

Awain gathered his first and said, "Since we can't find the sacred beast's location, we should probably let Spinel swim for a bit longer instead of arresting her. You said the next deal would be in three days, correct?"

"Yes, Spirit King. I'm sure that is what the man said," Ruri answered.

"In that case, we'll apprehend Spinel *and* the perpetrator then. In the meantime, I'll collect all the evidence and get everything in order."

"I'll help as well!" Ruri volunteered, brimming with enthusiasm.

Awain smiled wryly at her. "While I appreciate the offer, I must decline."

"Huh?!"

"This is a matter for the Nation of the Spirit King. I cannot allow a Beloved—another nation's Beloved, at that—to get wrapped up in anything dangerous."

"Aww, wha?" Ruri said, her overwhelming excitement starting to deflate.

Jade chimed in, "Ruri, what Awain says is right."

"Come on. Not *you* too, Jade-sama."

"*I agree as well,*" Rin stated. "*You don't know what would happen seeing as how even Kotaro can't track our guy down.*"

Kotaro added, "*Yes, I am also in agreement.*"

Ruri slumped in disappointment. Nevertheless, because she would feel sorry if she were to inconvenience the Nation of the Spirit King by being part of an incident, she decided to obediently pull back.

15 The Rescue

"I'm...so...*booored*!" Ruri complained as she lay around in bed.

It had been three days since the meeting between Spinel and the mysterious man had happened, which meant that today was the day of the deal. It was assumed that the exchange would go down at night, just like last time, so Ruri and the other Beloveds were sequestered in their rooms. There were more guards than usual outside Ruri's room, and Kotaro had put a powerful barrier up too. They were armed to the teeth. It was almost like they were asking anyone to come if they dared.

In contrast to the tense surroundings, Ruri was taking things easy. This was mostly because she trusted Kotaro and the other spirits. Jade, on the other hand, was still being overprotective. Seemingly still worried despite the strict security in place, he hadn't left Ruri's side since this morning. Given that this was an issue for the Nation of the Spirit King, Jade had no choice but to keep himself out of their affairs and wait for the nation's people to solve it.

It had been suggested that they both return to the Nation of the Dragon King, but now that Ruri was suspected of being the culprit, leaving the Nation of the Spirit King before the case wrapped up could be construed as her running away. The consensus was that it was best to trust in the Nation of the Spirit King to catch the culprit since they knew that Spinel was the ringleader.

Be that as it may, because Awain couldn't frivolously disclose his nation's internal affairs, he hadn't given Jade any real details, and Ruri could tell that Jade was getting impatient. Still, she was a Beloved, and Kotaro, the supreme-level Spirit of Wind, was by her side. Even if Awain wouldn't speak directly, everything he said was fair game to the spirits of the wind. The concept of privacy didn't exist.

Kotaro sorted through the information that the spirits had been gathering and relayed it to Ruri.

"It appears that they've done some thorough investigation on that girl. She doesn't seem to be any the wiser, though."

"Did they find out anything?" Ruri asked as she lay belly down on the bed with her arms stretched out.

"It seems that most of this has been coming from that girl's mother rather than the girl herself."

"Aah, Spinel's mother—the one who made her believe that Jade-sama was coming for her. Lapis said that she tried to get him to take her daughter as his first wife too, if I recall."

As Ruri and Kotaro continued to converse, Jade, who had been restlessly pacing around the room, sat next to Ruri as she lay on the bed and combed his fingers through her hair, making her grin.

"You should try to take it easy, Jade-sama. We won't accomplish anything if we're on edge."

Jade remained silent for a moment before letting out a small sigh and flopping down beside Ruri.

Ruri grinned in satisfaction, then urged Kotaro to continue. "So *what* exactly came from the mother?"

"Old pieces of documentation—one that details how a sacred beast's heart crystallizes after its death and the process for mixing an elixir that uses it as an ingredient. It would seem that she pilfered those documents, which are only passed down to the head of the House of Morga."

"And he never caught on that they were stolen?"

"*Apparently not.*"

Ruri and Jade both looked disappointed. Spinel was bad, but neither could shake the feeling that the head of the House of Morga had a host of issues of his own. It made them wonder how he even managed to continue being the leader of the head nobles. Then again, perhaps he was too busy to be mindful of the happenings within his family—a common occurrence for a standard workaholic.

"*Also, the mother was the one who proposed assassinating the sacred beast—my current body. She even eliminated the caretaker who poisoned it.*"

"Whoa… That's guilty if I ever heard it," Ruri remarked. "But I thought that Spinel was the one who did that. She said so herself."

"*I suppose the mother planned it, and the daughter carried it out.*"

Jade interjected, "But how did those two do that on their own? The caretaker was captured and jailed, wasn't he? How could they kill someone inside there?"

"*As for that, I would venture that they used sorcery.*"

"Sorcery? You mean *witchcraft* sorcery?" asked Jade.

"*No. Just because it's sorcery doesn't necessarily mean it's from witches,*" Kotaro explained. "*The witches' brand of sorcery was referred to as such because they could use magic to curse and mystify people. Even regular humans can use magic that inflicts curses upon people. You too, Ruri, if you had the knowledge.*"

"Oh, I see," Ruri replied. She wasn't sure if she *wanted* to use something like that even if she could.

"*Trees shares my opinion. It would be impossible to slip past his watchful eye otherwise. Although…if the person who killed the caretaker*" *and the person who kidnapped the missing sacred beast are one and the same, that would be a different story. And they actually did slip past both me and Trees to kidnap the pup in the first place."*

"So, basically…Spinel and her mother planned things out, but we won't know who the real perpetrator is until we apprehend whoever kidnapped the cub."

"That is the gist of things."

"So we'll have to wait after all," Jade lamented.

"But they apprehended the mother not long ago. They're still letting the daughter swim, though."

"Well, that's good news," said Ruri.

All they had to do now was wait until nightfall.

As that thought was settling in, Jade suddenly sprung up.

"What's the matter, Jade-sama?" Ruri prodded.

Jade walked to the window and threw it open, a stern expression on his face.

Ruri had a bad feeling and asked, "What's wrong?"

"Animal cries. And they're getting closer and closer."

"Huh?"

Ruri sat up and looked out the window, but she couldn't hear anything. Confused, she peeled her eyes from Jade and turned to Kotaro.

"Hmm, the sacred beasts are making noise. They've left the forest, and they're about to head toward the castle."

"How come?"

"They are coming out to look for the missing pup. They scoured the forest but didn't find anything. They must have lost patience when the Spirit King didn't send any news of the discovery. This is the second time that the sacred beasts have lost one of their young. All of them have left the forest in order to search on their own."

"Um, that's bad, isn't it?" asked Ruri.

"*I would suppose,*" Kotaro replied.

The sacred beasts were born sheltered, living in the forest under the Spirit of Trees's protection. They were just as special to the Nation of the Spirit King as spirits were, and it would probably incite a massive panic if they left the forest.

At that moment, a voice suddenly descended upon them.

"*Wind.*"

"*Hmm, is that you, Trees?*"

"*Could I ask you to stop them?*"

"*You want me to?*"

"*It would be more significant if you did it because you have a sacred beast's body. Plus, they're also of the wind. Being the Spirit of Wind, you are the most suited for the task.*"

"*Hmm. That is true, but...*" Kotaro trailed off, looking at Ruri. He was reluctant to leave her side.

"I'll be fine, Kotaro. You should go," Ruri assured him.

After thinking it over for a bit, Kotaro figured that since Jade and the other spirits would be around, Ruri would be safe.

"*Okay, then,*" Kotaro agreed.

"*Thank you. I appreciate your help,*" said the Spirit of Trees.

"*Mm-hmm,*" Kotaro replied before jumping out the window. He landed softly on the ground and dashed toward the source of the commotion.

"Hmm, I wonder if he'll be okay," Ruri muttered.

"*We'll just have to stay put and leave it to Kotaro,*" Rin said, no sign of panic in her voice. She even began to have a drink on the table.

Rin's behavior instantly relaxed Ruri.

Jade asked her, "Do you want something to drink, Ruri?"

"Yes, I'd like something warm, if that's okay," Ruri replied.

"Got it," he said, ringing the bell on the table. A servant immediately entered the room, and Jade ordered drinks for two.

Ruri was staring out the window with her back turned to both of them when she suddenly heard a sound—less of a sound and more of a cry. She turned to look behind her, but all she saw was Jade talking to the servant, unaware of the sound. She turned back to look out the window, and something caught her eye. She looked up with a gasp to find a brown-skinned man meeting eyes with her.

"Oh crap!" the man whispered.

Ruri stood stock still and stared at him blankly. She had met this man somewhere before. As she tried to recall who he was, she caught sight of something tied to his back—the sacred beast pup.

"Aaah!" Ruri shouted loudly and pointed.

"What's all the racket, Rur— Wha?!"

When Jade turned around, he saw a tan-skinned man holding Ruri in a full nelson. On the man's back was...the missing sacred beast.

They had expected it to be the same size as Kotaro, seeing how his body had also come from a sacred beast pup, but that wasn't the case at all. This pup was small enough to lift with one arm.

The fluffy white pup moaned sadly with an "ahung."

"So you're the kidnapper?! Unhand Ruri and the sacred beast!" Jade commanded, instantly switching into combat mode and pulling his sword from his pocket space.

The servant rushed out of the room without a moment's delay and called for backup. A pack of soldiers rushed into the room. The dragonkin, including Ewan and Finn, were naturally among them.

"Ruri! You got yourself caught *again*?!" Ewan carped.

Feeling extremely apologetic, Ruri tried to calmly assess the situation. "I've met you before, haven't I? At the market, if I remember correctly."

"Oh, you remember me? I recognized you right away. I could never forget a pretty girl like you," the tan-skinned man, Gibeon, said, as he kissed Ruri's hair.

Just then, a dagger whizzed by, grazing Ruri's locks.

"Whoa!" Gibeon shouted as he reflectively avoided the dagger. If he hadn't, it would have certainly stabbed him right in the face.

The thrower was none other than Jade, the man with the enraged demonic expression.

"Hey, that was dangerous, you," Gibeon said. "What woulda happened if you hit this cute girl?!"

"I wouldn't allow a single scratch to befall Ruri," Jade declared.

"Ah, right, right. Your name is Ruri. I remember your name now too. I'm Gibeon," he said, grinning up a storm as if he had no grasp of the situation.

Jade's anger, however, was at its peak. "Unhand Ruri *now*!"

"Hey, sure thing~! *If* you guys let me go."

"Nonsense! We can't let the abductor of a sacred beast go scot-free."

"Yup, I figured~! Then what if I did this?" Gibeon said and pointed a sharp dagger at Ruri's neck.

The tension in the room skyrocketed. While Jade froze, gritting his teeth as if he were going to click his tongue in frustration, Ruri remained composed. She grabbed the blade of the knife and twisted Gibeon's hand in the opposite direction with her free hand.

"Te-yah!" Ruri yelled.

"Gaah!" Gibeon cried in pain, his hand twisted at an angle it shouldn't have been.

With his hold now broken, Ruri easily ran back to Jade.

"R-Ruri?! Is your hand all right?!" Jade asked in a panic. After all, she'd gripped the blade of a dagger with her bare hands. It was only normal that he would be worried.

Ruri's hand was perfectly fine, though. She smiled at Jade and explained, "Kotaro has a strong barrier in place around me, so I wouldn't get wounded just from a knife touching me."

"I see. Thank goodness," Jade said, sighing in relief and hugging her tight.

Ruri tapped on his arms. "Now isn't the time."

"Yes, you're right." Jade let go of Ruri and primed his sword.

Even though Gibeon was trapped like a rat, he was grinning like a fool. "Oh boy, this is what it's like to face certain doom?"

"Come quietly and surrender," Jade commanded.

"Well, well… What should I do?" Gibeon trailed off and then quickly took the sacred beast from his back and chucked it at Ruri.

"Whoa, whoa, whoa!" Ruri scrambled to make the catch. She looked at the safe pup and breathed a sigh of relief.

Everyone, who'd been too distracted with the sacred beast, all at once remembered Gibeon and looked over to where he stood. Unfortunately, he'd disappeared without a trace.

"Wha?! Where did he go?!" Ruri interjected.

"Search for him! He couldn't have gone far!" Jade ordered.

The door and the window were the only escape routes. There was a mass of soldiers crowding the door, meaning the window was his only option. Yet he couldn't be seen from there.

"Where in the world did he go?" said a voice from the baffled crowd.

As everyone stood in confusion, someone parted the sea of soldiers and entered the room, holding a gigantic paper fan.

"Huh? The Spirit of Light?" asked Ruri.

"*Oh my, it is Light,*" Rin remarked.

While Ruri, Rin, and the members of the Nation of the Dragon King were baffled by the Spirit of Light's presence, the spirit took a look around the room and stopped at a certain spot. Everyone watched, curious as to what she was doing, when the Spirit of Light used the gigantic fan to smack the seemingly empty air. When she did, a loud thwack rang through the room and Gibeon was revealed, unconscious and with his eyes rolled back.

"Mm-hmm, that should do it," the Spirit of Light said, nodding in satisfaction. She slapped Gibeon's face, but he was out cold. "Okay, hurry up and restrain him."

Once Ruri and the others snapped out of their daze, the soldiers from the Nation of the Spirit King rushed over to Gibeon and started wrapping him with rope. You could feel their anger with each coil they wrapped around the young man. When they finished, they carted Gibeon straight out of the room.

The room was now cleared, and only those from the Nation of the Dragon King remained. It felt like the aftermath of a storm.

"Why are you here, Spirit of Light?" Ruri inquired.

"Because Wind kept asking me a bunch of weird questions. I came here to find out what he was talking about. Now I know the reason. It seems like it was my fault. Sorry."

"*What do you mean?*" Rin asked, fluttering up to her.

"We can talk about that later. Anyway, shouldn't you hurry up and get that back to its parents?" the Spirit of Light suggested, pointing her paper fan at the sacred beast child.

"Oh, true. The sacred beasts are going to leave the forest and come here if we don't return it soon!" Ruri exclaimed.

She was only thinking about getting the pup back to the forest, so she bolted out of the room in a hurry.

"Ruri!" Jade shouted, but it fell on deaf ears.

Rin fluttered out of the room in pursuit of her. She landed on Ruri's shoulder as Ruri ran through the castle at top speed.

"*Come now, Ruri. You can't just run recklessly about because you have Kotaro's barrier around you. The king was worried sick.*"

"Aha ha, sorry. I let the feeling of safety get to my head," Ruri replied, explaining why she'd ended up forgetting that she was a Beloved—a protected person. Dreading the stern talking-to that she would undoubtedly get later, Ruri kept running.

"*Ruri~! Turning here is a shortcut~!*"

"*Yup!*"

"Thanks!"

The spirits, who had been chasing her like Rin, gave Ruri directions. She raced down the hallway and exited out into the gardens. Just as she was about to cut through the courtyard, she heard someone call out to her, causing her to slam on the brakes.

"Hold it!" the person yelled.

Ruri turned around, wondering who would've stopped her in such a rush, only to find Spinel peering back at her.

"I insist that you hand over that sacred beast."

Ruri shook her head, replying, "I'm going to return this pup back to its parents."

"Then I will do it. I cannot allow you, an individual from another nation, to be bothered with such a task. I shall take responsibility and bring it back to its home."

Ruri couldn't believe how Spinel was able to deliver those lines so brazenly. Of course, Ruri wasn't going to give the pup to her since she knew that Spinel was involved in its kidnapping.

"No way. If I give it to you, you're just going to use it as an ingredient in your *elixir*," Ruri sarcastically replied.

Spinel's hands shook. "Whatever are you talking about? An elixir? What do you mean?"

Ruri and Rin looked at Spinel with cold eyes.

"You can stop playing dumb," Ruri said. "I know everything. The man you were cutting a deal with has already been arrested, and I'm sure they'll be coming to arrest you next."

Spinel gritted her teeth. "That's even more reason for you to hand the sacred beast over to me!" she screamed, pouncing at Ruri.

Ruri quickly dodged her advances and tightened her grip around the pup to protect it. "There's no way I would just say, 'oh sure, here you go,' and hand it over!"

Spinel grabbed Ruri's arm and dug her nails in, but thanks to Kotaro's barrier, Ruri's skin remained unscratched. However, when Spinel tugged on Ruri's hair, she pulled out a few hairs.

Ruri cried out in pain—maybe the barrier didn't extend all the way to her hair— but she wasn't going to relinquish the pup under any circumstances.

The onlooking spirits, beside themselves in rage, came in to rescue Ruri. They slowly closed in on Spinel, who was none the wiser.

"The time for punishment has come!"

"Punishment!"

"Punish herrr!"

The spirits latched on to Spinel and kept her from moving. Spinel had no idea what was happening since she couldn't see any of them, and she fell into a panic.

"Eeek! What?! What's going on?!" Spinel screamed as a mountain of spirits so large that not even Ruri knew where they'd all come from crushed her and brought her to her hands and knees. Looking down at Spinel on the ground, Ruri asked, "What did you plan on doing with the elixir? Were you going to use it on Jade-sama?"

Spinel looked up at Ruri with disdain. "Of course, I have no choice! My mother said that I would need the elixir in order to secure Master Jade's heart!"

"Again with your mother, huh?" Ruri said, her words tinged with exasperation. "So, what? Would you be satisfied with controlling Jade-sama with an elixir? Wouldn't that be a hollow victory?"

"It has *nothing* to do with you!" Spinel snapped back.

"It has *everything* to do with me! You've been lying about me and damaging my reputation!" Ruri replied as the spirits all nodded and puffed their chests in agreement.

"It's your fault. You're trying to steal Master Jade away from me! *I* am to be Master Jade's wife! My mother told me that he would be coming to take my hand. I have been waiting for him this entire time!" Spinel proclaimed. Her words were born of unjust resentment, and she looked at Ruri with hate in her eyes.

Ruri, on the other hand, felt that Spinel looked pathetic and rather undeserving of her anger.

"Is that *your* idea?" Ruri asked.

Spinel, confused, replied, "Huh?"

"You want the elixir because your mother told you. You waited for Jade-sama because your mother told you. Mother, mother, *mother*. Your mother tells you *everything*. Where does that leave *you*, then?"

"Wh-What are you talking about?"

"You haven't figured it out yet? Okay, then, would you have tried to get the sacred beast if your mother hadn't told you to do so? What do you know of Jade-sama *besides* what your mother told you?"

Spinel seemed to be at a loss for words.

"What, can't answer? How come? You're going to be Jade-sama's wife, aren't you? Why don't you know anything about him? Wouldn't a person normally want to know about the man they're in love with?"

"Well…"

"You were just your mother's puppet in the end, weren't you?"

"N-No! No, no, no!" Spinel refuted, repeating herself like a broken record. It looked like she was doing that to hold herself together.

Ruri was suddenly hit with a hollow feeling. When she thought about all of the things that this girl had put her through, her anger deflated.

"So, the mother was the root of evil," Ruri said to herself, hoping that Awain would give Spinel's mother a harsh punishment.

Just then, the dragonkin, led by Ewan, came running up.

"Hey, Ruri! Is this where you were?!" Ewan inquired. "We were looking all over for you!"

"Ah, sorry, sorry. Hey, would you mind delivering this girl to the Spirit King for me?"

The dragonkin looked down at Spinel on the ground next to Ruri. Ewan, who couldn't see spirits, was confused, but the other dragonkin grimaced.

"I'm heading to where Kotaro is," Ruri informed them.

"I'll come with you," offered Ewan.

Leaving them to drag Spinel out of the pile of spirits, Ruri headed for Kotaro with Ewan and Rin in tow. There, near the border of the forest, Kotaro was trying to persuade the sacred beasts to wait. The sacred beasts looked bloodthirsty, and the faces of the Nation of the Spirit King's soldiers were all tense.

"Kotaro!" Ruri called out.

"*Ruri*," Kotaro replied in a tone that suggested a spirit had filled him in beforehand. He didn't seem the least bit surprised to see Ruri carrying the small sacred beast.

"Aroof, aroof," howled the pup.

The once-bloodthirsty beasts crowded around Ruri. Their eyes were now calm, and they looked at the child as relief started to fill the air. Ruri gently set the sacred beast child down on the ground. It wagged its tiny tail happily and greeted each and every one of its elders with a touch of the tip of its nose. The sacred beasts began to return to the forest, the child in the center of the pack.

"Well, that solves that problem," said Ruri.

Just as Ruri was feeling satisfied, Ewan gave Ruri a firm chop to the head. He was holding back, of course, but it still hurt, nonetheless.

"Hey, what was that for, Ewan?" she howled.

"You need to get more used to being protected. Otherwise, *we'll* wind up in trouble!"

"Yeah, but…"

"No *buts*!"

"Okay, I'm sorry…" Ruri meekly apologized, knowing that excuses wouldn't work on the angry Ewan.

16 The Man Known as Gibeon

With the culprit apprehended and the sacred beast returned to the forest, the case came to a close, and everyone lived happily ever after—only things hadn't ended that easily. The head noble's second wife and their daughter had not only been involved in the recent kidnapping, but they'd also instigated the poisoning incident as well; the effects were immeasurable. The House of Morga was going to be in a very awkward position. Then again, that was none of Ruri and the others' concern since they were from another nation.

The Spirit King wouldn't explain the nation's inner workings in much detail, but that was where Kotaro, the supreme-level Spirit of Wind, came into play. According to the information Kotaro had gathered, Spinel and her mother had been interrogated after their arrest. The mother was apparently making an unabashed ruckus despite being in custody, but Spinel was obediently answering their questions. Ruri thought that she'd been a little too harsh on Spinel, but there were some things that you should and shouldn't do, so Ruri had no regrets.

From Spinel and her mother's accounts, Ruri got the general idea of the series of events. It had all started when the sacred beast was poisoned. Spinel's mother had triggered that incident to set Jade up to marry Spinel. Her plan had been to marry off her daughter, whom she considered beautiful, to a man of high social standing in order to gain more say in the House of Morga.

Originally, it had been Lapis who caught her eye. She'd thought that Lapis, given his lovesick disposition, would jump at the chance as soon as she introduced her daughter to him. Once the two exchanged vows, it would be in the bag. After all, Spinel was still young, and she was the daughter of the House of Morga. Figuring that Lapis wouldn't break a promise with the head noble's daughter, the mother had planned to make Spinel his first wife. Lapis, however, was not the least bit interested in a child like Spinel and had begun to run from the mother's forceful advances.

Realizing that her plans with Lapis were a bust, the mother had shifted to her next target—Jade. She'd convinced Spinel to believe in a promise that Jade had never made in order to make Spinel fall in love with Jade. It was safe to say that it was outright brainwashing. The mother proceeded to try and set up a time for Spinel and Jade to meet, but that proved very difficult. At the time, Jade was fed up with Agate and the other elders pestering him about a wife, so he wasn't letting any unmarried girls, or parents with unmarried daughters, near him.

As Spinel's mother ground her teeth in frustration, she just so happened to learn about the elixir. She'd dug around in her husband's room, which was always vacant since he rarely came back home, and learned how to make it. With this knowledge in hand, she'd used Spinel to cajole the sacred beast's caretaker into cooperating. Spinel had easily won over the earnest young man, and he'd done exactly as Spinel had instructed. To their dismay, though, the body of the sacred beast they'd managed to kill had been offered to Kotaro before they could get their hands on it. Also, the beast's caretaker had been arrested, prompting Spinel's mother to hire an assassin to kill him so he couldn't snitch.

Everyone was baffled about how the assassin had managed to kill the caretaker right under the Spirit of Trees's nose, but just as Kotaro had feared, the assassin was capable of hexing sorcery.

It was still a surprise that Spinel's mother had managed to conveniently find one such person, but it seemed to be just a coincidence. Unfortunately, the assassin was nowhere to be found, and the Nation of the Spirit King was currently searching for them. They *did* find the contract made with said assassin, though. The words "Request to Assassinate via Sorcery" were prudently written on the paper and even sealed with blood.

After eliminating the caretaker, Spinel's mother had heard that another sacred beast had been born recently. She turned to crime again because, in her mind, stealing a small pup would be even easier. The person she'd hired to carry out the kidnapping was Gibeon.

Ruri and the others decided to ask Gibeon about the kidnapping. Jade and Ruri were allowed to sit in on the interrogation as Gibeon himself claimed that the Spirit of Light was a participant. Gibeon, still wrapped in rope, struggled against his bonds as he sat on the floor, looking disgruntled. Ruri and the others sat down in chairs, and the interrogation began.

"That outfit of yours. That belongs to the Nation of Iolite, doesn't it?" Awain questioned.

Gibeon looked away from him and pouted.

Seeing his response, Lapis ordered the spirits, "Sic him."

"*Okay!*"

"*We'll get 'em!*"

The spirits delightfully surrounded Gibeon and began to tickle every nook and cranny of his body.

"Gaaaah!" Gibeon screamed.

While the young man suffered his punishment, Ruri asked Jade, "Jade-sama, wasn't the Nation of Iolite destroyed not too long ago?"

"Yes, it was," Jade replied.

"If he's dressed in those clothes, does that mean he's from that nation?"

"Well?" Jade asked Gibeon, throwing the question to the young man.

Gibeon replied in between labored breaths, "That's...right..."

"You broke into a restricted area and kidnapped a sacred beast at the request of the House of Morga's second wife and his daughter. That is indeed what you've done, is it not?" Awain questioned, reading off of a thoroughly written document he held in one hand.

Gibeon didn't respond.

"If you don't reply, you're gonna get it again," Lapis threatened.

Gibeon twitched in fear.

"I normally would have conducted a more proper torture," began Awain, "but I'll let you go with this since there's a lady present. Although, I'm more than willing to oblige if you would prefer something more intense."

Awain smirked deviously along with Lapis, which only heightened the sense of dread when coupled with the already scary glint in the pair's eyes. They were a duo with looks that could kill—quite literally.

Gibeon went pale.

"Yeah! That's right! You shouldn't be complaining at all!" Lapis commented.

"I still have more questions too. How exactly did you kidnap the sacred beast?" Awain asked with a sharp, pensive glare. "The Spirit of Trees protects the castle and the forest. You kidnapped the pup without the Spirit of Trees even noticing. How did you do that?"

Before Gibeon could answer, the Spirit of Light interrupted him. "I'll elaborate on that. After all, it seems I'm involved in it all."

"*Come to mention it, you did say that earlier. What did you mean by that?*" Rin inquired, flapping her wings and flying around the Spirit of Light.

"It was twenty-some years ago. I was in the Nation of Iolite before its collapse. I'd been following Quartz, who was looking for Seraphie's reincarnation at the time, and we visited Iolite. The queen of the nation took us in for a stint. When I asked her what I could do to thank her, she said that she wanted a blessing for her child. The queen was with child, it seemed. It was an easy request, so I obliged and blessed the unborn baby."

Ruri tilted her head, unsure of what that had to do with Gibeon, while Jade and Awain looked at Gibeon in shock.

"Don't tell me that the child from then is…" Jade started.

"Yes, it's the man sitting right there," replied the Spirit of Light.

That was enough for Ruri to understand as well. "Huh? So does that mean he's a *prince*?"

"Yes, indeed!" Gibeon replied in a chipper tone, an unfitting one given the tense stares he drew from everyone in the room.

"I never would have guessed that the same child I blessed would come to abuse it. In fact, I had completely forgotten I'd done that until I actually saw him," said the Spirit of Light with a slightly exasperated sigh.

"Erm, what is a 'blessing'?" Ruri asked unassumingly. "Is it different from the contract I have with Kotaro and Rin?"

Rin answered, "*I assume you already know how a contract works at this point. A blessing differs from a contract in that a spirit loans a portion of their powers. Those who receive a spirit's blessing can use the spirit's powers. There are also many other benefits, such as it being easier to use powers of that element.*"

"Oh wow," replied Ruri.

"*Still, I see now. It's no wonder that Trees couldn't find him, much less Kotaro. With a barrier deployed using Light's powers, he could hide himself and infiltrate the castle without being detected by anyone, the spirits included.*"

"Pretty amazing, isn't it?" Gibeon said proudly with his chest puffed out.

Lapis, irritated with Gibeon's behavior, slapped Gibeon across the head—an act that most likely spoke for everyone present.

Awain pressed his fingers against his temples as if he felt a headache coming on. "I see. Well, that explains *how* he did it. But *why* would the prince of Iolite do such a thing in the first place?" he asked. Even though the nation was defunct, there had to be a reason the former prince would commit such a crime.

"My homeland was destroyed a while back, and the neighboring nation executed the royal family—including my parents. I was the only one who managed to escape, but up until that point, I'd been a sheltered and pampered little boy. I had to get my hands dirty in order to survive. I did everything I could. I was part of a pirate crew not too long ago, but I remember hearing that those same pirates were taken out trying to raid the Nation of the Dragon King's ship just recently. I'm pretty darn lucky, don'tcha think?"

Gibeon seemed to be referring to the pirates whom Ruri's crew had encountered on the way to the Nation of the Spirit King. Ruri looked at Jade to confirm this, but he wasn't sure either.

"I still can't believe a former *prince* would turn to being a *pirate*," Awain said, looking disappointed.

"I'm all too aware that it's quite random. But what other choice did I have? I was taught how to be a king, but never how to be a commoner. What *should* I have done?" Gibeon replied, staring at Awain with innocent eyes.

"Yes, you're right. That was a tad thoughtless of me," Awain admitted.

No one present could ever understand Gibeon's suffering. No one could comprehend the feelings of being forced to sully their hands in order to survive.

It was common sense that criminal acts were wrong. Even so, words like that seemed entirely hypocritical to Gibeon. No matter what he heard from people who lived without needing to worry about the bare necessities, it wouldn't touch him in the slightest. Still, while there were reasons to sympathize with Gibeon's situation, it didn't erase the fact that he'd kidnapped a sacred beast.

Awain seemed to be at a loss for what to do. "In the Nation of the Spirit King, sacred beasts are just as important a symbol as spirits. Kidnapping one is a serious crime. Therefore, you will be banished from the country and never allowed to set foot in this nation again."

Gibeon was surprised. "Are you serious? That's pretty much like acquitting me," he said. Since he wasn't originally from this nation, banishment was barely a slap on the wrist.

"I will send out an official decree later. Until then, you will remain confined and reflect on your actions. Take him away," Awain ordered.

"Sire!" replied the soldiers as they dragged Gibeon, who looked to be in disbelief, away.

Once Gibeon was gone, Awain heaved a heavy, exhausted sigh.

"Are you sure about this?" Jade asked him.

"Yes, because no one got hurt this time around. If he'd been involved in the previous poisoning incident or damage had accrued during this incident, then it would have been a different story. However, it seems the abducted pup was treated with care—so much care that it's begged to play with Gibeon sometime again. My head hurts just thinking of how to handle *that* situation.

"Plus," Awain continued, "if he is the prince of the Nation of Iolite, that's even more reason to be careful how I punish him. The country itself is gone now, but the Iolitians are still alive and well.

If the Nation of the Spirit King were to severely punish the prince of Iolite, then the former Iolitians might lash back. That nation already has enough pent-up resentment from its downfall. I would say that deporting him is a fitting compromise."

"Ah, I see," replied Jade.

"I'm sorry that I embroiled you all in this nation's affairs," Awain apologized. "I'm especially sorry for the trouble we've caused you, Ruri."

Ruri waved her hand and said, "Oh, no worries. It was just a few rumors spread about me."

"I'm glad to hear you say that. Allow me to make it up to you by treating you all to as much food and drink as you please."

"I'm humbled, but might I suggest that you keep Celestine-san's alcohol consumption to a minimum?" Ruri quipped, causing everyone who knew of Celestine's drinking habits to chuckle heartily.

The New Resident

A dinner party was held for the rulers of the four nations and their Beloveds. With the Nation of the Spirit King's recent issues squared away and the original purpose of the meeting concluded, all that was left was for the guests to return to their respective lands.

Ruri had suspected that everyone would cut loose a little at the party, but her fears came to fruition when a drunken Celestine decided to confront her.

"It's not too late. Give me Master Jade's dragonheart!"

"It's impossible, I tell you. I've long since swallowed it," Ruri replied.

"Spit it out!" Celestine demanded.

"Don't be absurd!" Ruri retorted.

Celestine gulped down her glass of wine and tried to pour another glass, but Ruri stopped her before she could.

"Come on, now. You're drinking too much, Celestine-san," Ruri scolded, prying the wine bottle from Celestine's hands.

Unfortunately, that only made Celestine even more confrontational. "Give that back! You're not only going to steal Master Jade, but my alcohol as well?!"

"Your eyes are all glazed over! Here, drink this!" Ruri handed Celestine a glass of water, which Celestine obediently took and began sipping.

"This wine has no flavor," Celestine remarked.

"It's a new type of wine that's all the rage nowadays~!" Ruri said, making up a story. Celestine bought it, though, and continued drinking from the glass.

Ruri was overcome with relief now that Celestine had calmed down, but then she noticed that two people had been watching their exchange with smiles.

"Jade-sama, Beast King, would it kill either of you to stop her?"

"Hey, I already babysit her enough on the regular, so cut me some slack today, all right?" Arman replied.

Not even attempting to come to the rescue, Jade added, "And if I were to jump in, Celestine would raise even more of a fuss, wouldn't she?"

Ruri looked out at the others. Adularia was silently sipping her wine like a refined adult. Meanwhile, Lapis, who was just as drunk as Celestine, was so loopy that he was starting to take off his clothes. Fortunately, Awain scolded him and stopped him before he could.

"Let me strip~!" Lapis cried.

"Will you stop it, you foolish excuse for a son!" Awain exclaimed.

Awain seemed to be having a tough time controlling his inebriated son. Having dealt with a drunken Celestine a number of times now, Ruri sympathized with him greatly.

"Ruri, are you sure you don't want to drink?" Jade asked.

"I'm going to pass for today," Ruri answered. "I plan on going into town early tomorrow morning, after all."

"You never told me that," Jade said, his brow furrowing.

"Oh, I didn't? Well, yes, I'm going to buy some souvenirs for everyone waiting back home. I'll have Ewan accompany me, so I'll be fine."

"Why not just have me, your *husband*, take you instead?"

"Because you seem busy enough with your own business. You still need to broker that deal with the boat, don't you?"

The purchase negotiations with the Nation of the Spirit King and the Imperial Nation for the Nation of the Dragon King's ship, a magic tool that Seraphie had crafted, was set for tomorrow. Ruri was trying to be considerate and plan around that, but it seemed to only displease Jade.

"I'll make sure to buy a souvenir for you too, Jade-sama," Ruri added.

"That *isn't* the point!" Jade insisted.

"Lady Ruri!" Celestine cried. "Are you flirting with Master Jade *agaaain*?!"

"Ah, here, here. Another new type of wine~!"

Ruri passed Celestine some more water, and Celestine once again began taking tiny sips. Ruri then spent the rest of the night trying to improve Jade's mood and taking care of the drunken Celestine.

The next day, Ruri went into town with the spirits, Ewan, and a few guards. She'd tried to invite Celestine and Lapis before she left the castle, but they'd both seemed to be too hungover to get out of bed. Ruri knew she'd made the right decision to not touch a drop of alcohol yesterday.

After Ruri looked around the many stores and bought a variety of souvenirs, she returned to the castle and found an extremely satisfied Jade, Claus, and Finn waiting for her.

Ewan rushed to Finn and presented him with the souvenir he'd just purchased—keeping to his tried-and-true brother complex.

"You two seem to be in a good mood," Claus commented.

"Welcome back, Ruri," Jade greeted her.

"Thank you. Judging from your mood, I'm guessing that negotiations went well?"

"They did. We received a request for ten ships from the Nation of the Spirit King and the Imperial Nation."

"Oh, wow. That's great!"

"And that's not all," Claus added. "Just as we initially planned, we asked the Imperial Nation's nobles to stop interacting with our nation's Beloveds in exchange for a price cut. They agreed, so I doubt they will be coming up to you anymore."

"That is a great relief," said Ruri. "I wouldn't be able to handle any nobles hounding me on my own. I don't have a clue how to deal with those types."

"We made sure to voice our complaints about how their meddling caused one of our Beloveds to go missing."

Beryl was not missing, but it sounded more like a complaint if they said he was. They weren't lying either, since Beryl had left the kingdom due to the nobles' interference. Judging by how refreshed Jade and Claus looked, they must have *really* dug into them verbally. It almost made Ruri feel a little sorry for the Imperial Nation's nobles.

Now that the Nation of the Dragon King's group had finished its business in the Nation of the Spirit King, they decided to head back home the same way they came—by boat.

Ruri looked back at the great tree, visible from the harbor, then boarded the ship. The journey back home was peaceful—no pirate raids this time around—except...

"Wow, I never thought we'd ever meet again," said Gibeon as he held on to Ruri's hand. "This must be fate. I bet you feel the same way. We must be soul mates, bound by destiny to cross one another from our previous lives."

Gibeon's grip made Ruri desperately want to escape reality.

"Why are you here?" she asked.

"Well, because we're both bound by fate, of course," he replied.

186

"No, that's not what I meant. Weren't you kicked out of the nation?"

"Yep, and I'm currently *out* of that nation, as you can plainly see."

"Uh, well, true enough," Ruri said, admitting that he was indeed out of the Nation of the Spirit King because he was on their ship traveling to the Nation of the Dragon King. "Wait, are you coming to the Nation of the Dragon King? Why?"

"Mr. Dragon King invited me on this trip to his kingdom, and I accepted because I don't really have anywhere else to go. Plus, not only was I flattered by the king's feverish attempts at seduction, but I also realized that the Nation of the Dragon King is where you'll be, Ruri. So, basically, I'm your bona fide husband-approved lover."

"You are *not*!" someone shouted as they chopped Gibeon's hand with theirs, breaking his grip on Ruri. That someone was Jade, and he was glaring daggers at Gibeon. "I simply suggested that you come to our nation if you had nowhere else to go. I certainly did not *feverishly seduce* you, nor do I recall ever giving you permission to touch Ruri!"

"Oh, come on, no need to be bashful. I totally appreciate and get how you feel, Mr. Dragon King. But I'm into women, personally. Sorry."

"Wait a second. What kind of misconception are you trying to spark up?! I have a wife and her name is *Ruri*!"

"Don't you worry. I'll make sure to satisfy Ruri as her lover *just fine*."

"To hell with you!" Jade exclaimed, having run out of patience. He drew his sword and swung it at Gibeon, but the young man casually avoided the strike.

"So you want me to entertain not only Ruri, but yourself as well, Mr. Dragon King? My, I'm even getting men to fall head over heels for me. It's really not easy being *such* a heartthrob," Gibeon said in a playful manner. He took out a mirror and entranced himself with his reflection.

A vein popped on Jade's forehead as he watched this vain display. "I'll *kill* you…"

"Please calm down, Your Majesty!" Finn interjected, stopping Jade.

"Enough of your games, Gibeon!" Claus scolded.

As Jade struggled with Finn and Claus, his sword went flying toward Gibeon.

"Ah! Look out!" Ruri shouted.

However, the sword bounced right off Gibeon as soon as it touched him. Everyone looked on in disbelief as Gibeon casually explained, "I have the blessing of the Spirit of Light, so something like this won't injure me if I just put up a barrier."

A villainous smirk drew across Jade's lips. "So I see. Then I can play with you without fear of holding back. Try not to die." He picked his sword up from the ground, assumed his stance, and sprung at the young man.

"Wha?! No, no. I don't wanna!" Gibeon grimaced as he fled.

Jade gave chase, and Finn and Claus gave up trying to stop him. It ended up being a lively voyage back home.

When Ruri returned to the Nation of the Dragon King's capital, she visited Euclase's office with Jade and Gibeon.

Euclase greeted them, saying, "Welcome back, Your Majesty. And you as well, Ruri."

"Yes, thank you. Here you go, a souvenir for you, Euclase-san," Ruri said, handing Euclase lipstick that was popular in the Nation of the Spirit King.

Euclase happily accepted it. "Why, thank you."

Euclase, with their sweet smile, was a dazzling beauty. There was no way that Gibeon *wouldn't* be moved when faced with such a beautiful person. He knelt before Euclase and took their hand with a debonair expression.

"A pleasure to meet you, O beautiful madame. I am Ruri's lover, Gibeon, officially approved by Mr. Dragon King, but I wouldn't mind becoming your slave of love if you so desire."

"I see you've brought home yet another weird fellow, Ruri," Euclase remarked, shooting a disappointed look at Ruri.

"It wasn't me this time. It was *Jade-sama*," Ruri declared, pointing to Jade as if telling Euclase to direct any complaints to him.

"His Majesty?" Euclase repeated.

Jade made a very sour expression as he explained, "I may have had a tiny lapse in judgment. I would return him if I could, but he's been exiled and deported from the Nation of the Spirit King, so that isn't a viable option."

"Exiled and deported? What on earth did he do to earn that?"

Jade went on to summarize the incidents in the Nation of the Spirit King, the events leading up to Gibeon's deportation, and the sympathy Jade felt for him as he persuaded Gibeon to come with him back home.

"Your Majesty, I know he is a former prince, but do you not think that bringing back a criminal was a rash decision?" Euclase questioned.

"Yes, it was. And I wholeheartedly regret it now," Jade admitted.

Gibeon buried his face in hands, hiding from the verbal shellacking they were giving him. "You're terrible. It's not like I wanted to live that way myself."

He appeared to be crying, but everyone knew they were crocodile tears. Nonetheless, there were parts of his story that deserved their sympathy.

"Well, he seems to be sorry for his actions, so why not hire him to work in the castle?" Ruri suggested, figuring that it would be better than letting him out to cause problems. Still, Ruri in no way trusted Gibeon.

Gibeon, on the other hand, was ecstatic about Ruri's suggestion. "Ruri!" he cried. "You truly *are* my soul mate! Leave it to me. I will do my best as your lover!"

Gibeon approached Ruri with his arms extended, but Jade stopped him just in the nick of time. "Ruri doesn't *need* a lover while I'm around. And I would never allow such a thing in the first place! You're to perform odd jobs for Euclase!"

"Huh? But I'd rather be Ruri's lover~!"

"Absolutely *not*! Ruri is *mine*!"

"They say that no girl likes a possessive guy. You need to be open-minded enough to allow her at least one lover," argued Gibeon.

"She doesn't need one!" Jade screamed in a rare display of open hostility.

Jade was essentially a pacifist, but that didn't seem to apply to insects clinging to his mate. Meanwhile, Ruri wished that Jade would release her from his extremely tight embrace.

In the end, it was settled that Euclase would take Gibeon into their care. Gibeon complained until the bitter end, but he appeared to be satisfied to work with such a beautiful young lady. Ruri decided to keep quiet about how that beautiful young lady was actually a beautiful young man. It was likely that Gibeon would lose all motivation to work if he were to find out.

After pretty much pushing Gibeon off on Euclase, Ruri and Jade went to Jade's office. Quartz was there, sitting in Jade's chair and taking care of Jade's kingly duties in his stead.

"Welcome back, Jade, Ruri," Quartz greeted them.

"Thank you very much for taking care of things while I was away, Master Quartz," Jade said.

"I was surprised to hear the Spirit of Light say that she was going to the Nation of the Spirit King, but I assume everything turned out fine?"

"It did. In fact, we solved our issue thanks to her help."

"I'm glad to hear that. But what's this I hear about Ruri bringing back a lover?" Quartz asked with a teasing smile.

Jade's mood immediately went downhill. Ruri wondered who'd told Quartz, but then she saw the Spirit of Light already in the room, sipping tea on the couch. She'd apparently filled Quartz in to a certain degree while Ruri and the others were talking in Euclase's office.

"You've made quite the interesting acquisition. I'll go say my regards later," Quartz said.

"It's not interesting at all," Jade grumbled.

"Even so, Ruri seems to be just fine with it. Ha ha ha," Quartz joked with a chuckle, but Jade found it to be no laughing matter.

"That reminds me," Jade said, looking at Ruri with a dour, criticizing glare, "you *did* say that guys like him were your type, didn't you, Ruri?"

"Aah, that's no good," Quartz remarked. "At times like this, you should have a nice, nuanced discussion with each other. In the *bedroom*."

Jade nodded at Quartz's advice. "So I see. A nuanced discussion…" he repeated.

Ruri felt that she was in danger for some reason and slowly started moving back. "Wait, wait, Jade-sama. You're not supposed to touch me until the tuning is over."

"Yes, that's right…"

Jade grasped Ruri's hand to keep her from fleeing. When he did, she felt something warm flow into her. She realized that Jade was sending mana into her for the dragonheart tuning, but it seemed different from usual. She could feel her chest getting hot, then the heat collected in one spot, making her wince.

Jade panicked and asked, "Ruri, what's wrong?"

"Oh, could it be…" Quartz started. He was the only one remaining composed and the only one knowledgeable about what was happening.

The heat that had built in Ruri's body suddenly started to die down. Jade was relieved to see Ruri up and about as if nothing had happened, but both were equally confused by what had transpired.

Quartz suddenly clapped his hands and said, "Congratulations, Ruri, Jade. It seems you've finished the tuning process."

"Is that what just happened?" asked Ruri.

"You should have proof of it somewhere on your body," Quartz explained.

"Somewhere?"

Ruri was checking her hands and her face when Jade took her hand and guided it to her neck.

"Right here, Ruri," Jade said.

Ruri touched her neck and felt something hard. She pulled a hand mirror from her pocket space and saw a scale the same color as Jade's eyes there.

"A scale the color of the dragonheart appearing somewhere on your body is proof that the tuning process is complete," explained Quartz.

"Oh wow, so this is what that means?" Ruri mused, looking at the scale in adoration...until Jade suddenly scooped her up.

Ruri's eyes widened as Jade looked at her with a virile smile. "If I recall, the agreement was that I could kiss you once the tuning was done, correct?"

Ruri's face sagged as an unbelievable feeling of dread sank into her.

"Master Quartz, I'd like you to act as interim king for a little while longer, please, if you would," Jade said.

"That's just fine. Leave it to me," Quartz replied with a thumbs-up and a smile stretching from ear to ear.

Jade flashed a smile of his own in response and walked off toward his quarters with Ruri in his arms.

The following day, when Ruri was finally set free, she made a mental note to *never* make Jade jealous ever again.

 **Epilogue**

"That was such an *ordeal...*"

After Jade had finally released Ruri from his clutches, news of the tuning being complete had spread throughout the castle. When Agate and the other elders found out, they'd gone into hustle mode. They'd deemed it necessary to celebrate the occasion, so they'd made preparations for a party without Ruri's permission. Ruri had never been more embarrassed in her entire life, but no one could stop the out-of-control old men and their skyrocketing excitement.

The lavish festivities were held a few days later. Once Ruri gave in and joined the impromptu party, everyone showered her with congratulations. After all, now that the tuning was complete, Ruri was fully initiated into the dragonkin ranks. She now aged much more slowly, and her body was much stronger than a human's—but still weaker than a dragonkin's. Ruri didn't really feel the results yet herself, but she figured she'd most likely start experiencing them, little by little, over time.

While Ruri was enjoying the party, Euclase called out to her.

"Ruriii!" Euclase said and handed her a letter. "It's from Master Beryl."

"Grandpa?"

Ruri hurriedly opened the letter to see a single photo inside. Apparently, Beryl had brought an instant camera with him to this world.

The photo was of Beryl smiling together with Chi on some sort of beach. He'd probably gone fishing, because he was carrying a gigantic fish in his arms—big enough to swallow him in one gulp. It seemed as though Beryl was very much enjoying his stay in this world.

"Nice, looks like grandpa is doing well," Ruri remarked.

"That is good to hear. We were worried that we didn't give enough attention to Master Beryl, so that is quite the relief," Euclase said. "Also, I must say that Gibeon has taken to his job like a fish to water. He may be a former prince of a now-defunct nation, but he is a prince through and through. He must have received a proper imperial education in the ways of running a kingdom. I'm amazed that he's so quick on the uptake, actually. It baffles me as to why he would turn to a life of crime when he is so capable. Then again, he is still going through his probation period to test his trustworthiness, so I can't allow him to handle anything too important, but I would say he's a great acquisition."

Once Ruri and Euclase finished their conversation, Euclase walked off. Ruri then went to find her parents, who were attending the party as well, and approached them with the photo in hand. Once they saw the photo, both of her parents started giggling, happy that Beryl was enjoying himself.

"Honestly speaking, our old world was way too constrictive for people with mana like us," Riccia said. "We can see the unseen. We can use power invisible to the naked eye. It was hard trying to lead a life while keeping all of that secret. I would assume that dad must feel positively liberated. I share the sentiment. Anyway, I wouldn't worry about it too much, Ruri." With a motherly expression, she patted Ruri on the head, assuming that Ruri was feeling guilty.

Ruri was worried that she'd gotten her family embroiled in this mess because she'd ended up in this world. She'd be lying if she said she didn't feel that way, but looking at Beryl's smiling face in this photo made her feel silly for continuing to worry about it. After all, Beryl and her parents were enjoying what this world had to offer. It was easier said than done, though.

"I'm sorry," Ruri said, apologizing for dragging her family into this situation, even though it was far too late for that. It was a shame that she couldn't apologize to Beryl in person, but she was confident that he would come back soon with an unruly amount of tales from his travels under his belt. Ruri might have a child by then as well. Knowing Beryl, he would no doubt play with them the best he could. She couldn't help but to look forward to that.

"I'm so glad I came here," Riccia professed. "Plus, it helped me find my life's mission—revolutionizing the clothing industry in this world. You should come over and help me if you're ever free, Ruri. I wouldn't mind at all if you were to help by working as a model."

"Riccia's store didn't see much business at first, but she's building a core fanbase and is busier than ever nowadays. So much so that she doesn't have enough staff on hand," Kohaku explained.

"Heat-sama is helping out too, isn't he?" asked Ruri.

"Yes, he sure is," replied Riccia.

Ruri looked doubtful. "Is he taking the job seriously?"

Heat was a spirit, a being who operated under a different logic than humans. He lived in a world divorced from concepts such as labor. Not to mention, it was hard to believe that someone like Heat, whose mind was only occupied by women, would be a diligent worker. In fact, even as they spoke, Heat was in the middle of hitting on the servant women.

Gibeon eventually joined the mix, and after Heat and he had a rather involved conversation, Gibeon pleaded, "Please let me call you 'teacher'!"

Looking satisfied with the prospect of having an underling, Heat arrogantly replied, "Very well, then."

The two womanizers were hitting it off.

"Heat-chan is doing his job. He's also been helping with advertising by being a model," Riccia trilled.

Ruri couldn't believe that Heat was practically dancing in the palm of her mother's hand. "Mom, do you know Heat-sama's weakness or something?" she asked.

"Tee hee hee," Riccia answered with a suggestive giggle, ultimately leaving the matter to remain a mystery.

When Ruri walked away from her parents, people came up and offered her drinks left and right. This was supposed to be a celebration for her, but she had the sinking suspicion that everyone just wanted to drink. Since all the guests were pounding back way more alcohol than what they offered her, it was hard to say *who* was the star of the party—her or the booze. Nevertheless, Ruri was having fun seeing everyone enjoy themselves.

Eventually, Ruri got light-headed from drinking, so she went to the garden in order to sober up. The breeze wafting across her skin felt great. She took a deep breath of the sea-infused air and exhaled. She could hear chattering and laughing off in the distance.

Ruri then walked away from the voices and headed toward Jade's office. She knocked, opened the door, and entered to find Jade hard at work.

"Jade-sama, are you sure you're not going to the party?" Ruri asked.

"I have too much work piled up that only I can sign off on. Besides, all they want is an excuse to drink. The Nation of the Dragon King's people love festivals and parties, after all. Especially dragonkin."

"That's true. Everyone has been drinking and having a ball without even realizing you're not around, Jade-sama."

"That's perfectly fine, so long as they don't destroy the castle."

"Isn't that a pretty tall order for them?"

Whenever they held a party where drinking was involved, it was practically guaranteed that the dragonkin would run amok and destroy the castle. Then, the following day, it was customary for them to repair things all over the place while recovering from their hangovers. They were probably destroying parts of the castle walls at this very moment.

"That reminds me," Ruri began, "I've never seen you in a drunken rampage before, Jade-sama."

"Of course you haven't. Someone is bound to stop the Dragon King if they go berserk."

"Surely."

The Dragon King was the strongest dragonkin of them all, so several dragonkin would need to pile on in order to contain him. Just the same, Ruri didn't want to see Jade act like that. His approval ratings would no doubt plummet.

With that in mind, Ruri figured it would be an issue if a Beloved went on a drunken rampage as well. She wished that Celestine would be more careful to preserve her image. As for Lapis, Awain normally scolded him when he got out of hand, which meant that Lapis probably wouldn't influence anyone around him. Ruri reminded herself to be careful as well.

After Jade finished navigating his paperwork, he put down his pen.

"Are you finished already?" Ruri asked.

"No, just taking a short break."

Jade stood up, took Ruri's hand, and moved over to the couch. He pulled some sandwiches from his pocket space and placed them on the table. He'd evidently had food prepared in advance since he had no intention of joining the party. Then he set Ruri on his lap.

This was Ruri's usual position, which was fine when she was in cat form, but it was slightly embarrassing when she was in human form and Jade's face was awfully close.

"Here you go, Ruri," Jade said, grabbing a bite-size sandwich and bringing it to Ruri's mouth. He watched in satisfaction as Ruri pushed her hair back behind her ear and took a bite.

On Ruri's exposed nape was a scale the same color as Jade's eyes—proof that the dragonheart had been tuned. Jade slowly leaned in and lovingly kissed the scale. After a long, confirming kiss, he looked at Ruri again and gently traced it with his finger.

"Jade-sama, you've been touching that spot a lot," Ruri commented. Jade had been continuously checking and touching her neck ever since the tuning was finished.

"Yes, because it's a mark that you are mine in the truest sense," Jade said, looking extremely happy.

Once she saw Jade's face, Ruri fell into a contented silence, but then she remembered. "Oh, right. My grandpa sent me a photo," she said, passing the picture to Jade.

"Your world has some useful tools. I wonder if we can make something similar…"

"Seraphie-san might be able to make one for us if we ask her."

"Hmm, Master Quartz would give me quite the dirty look if I were to occupy too much of Lady Seraphie's time."

"Well, yes, Quartz-sama *does* love Seraphie-san dearly."

"That is how male dragonkin operate. You should resign yourself to that, Ruri."

"Yes, yes," Ruri replied, already having done so. Or rather, she'd already "accepted" that fact.

"It seems that Lord Beryl is quite enjoying himself," Jade noted.

"Chi as well. I'm glad they're enjoying it like a vacation. Still, I'm positive that grandpa would be fine anywhere he went."

At first, Ruri had been surprised that Beryl had disappeared, leaving only a single letter behind, but once she thought about it rationally, she'd realized that there was nothing she needed to worry about. Beryl was a Beloved, and he had Chi and Andal with him. That was why, while she wasn't too concerned, she did feel relieved in a different way to actually see him safe and sound.

"Grandpa seems to be enjoying himself, so you don't need to worry too much either, Jade-sama," Ruri assured him, knowing that Jade felt guilty about Beryl leaving. Jade's aggressive tactics toward the Imperial Nation's nobles may have also been him taking out his frustrations. There was no need to worry, though, not with Beryl seeming to be having a blast in the photo.

"That's true. I've made the nobles of the Imperial Nation take responsibility. And if Lord Beryl doesn't think anything of it, then things are probably fine."

"Right, right. I'm sure he'll pop back home before long. And it seems that mom is enjoying herself as well, so I've decided to put it out of mind too."

"So I see."

Ruri paused, then murmured, "Now that I'm tuned, I'll be living a different kind of life from my parents and grandpa, won't I?"

"Yes… Do you regret it?" asked Jade.

She shook her head. "I do feel a tinge of sadness, but seeing grandpa and mom having the time of their lives makes me realize that I should stop thinking about what's yet to come and focus on enjoying the here and now. I don't want to regret the future."

"Did you omit Lord Kohaku from that on purpose?"

Ruri smirked. "Fair point. But my dad likes being wrapped around my mom's finger, so I think that he'll be fine so long as she's happy."

Ruri would have to part ways with them one day, but she wanted to enjoy the present and worry about the future later.

"I know I've said something similar in the past, but I will once again vow to you. I will be by your side to make up for the absence of your parents. Forever, till death do us part," Jade said, hugging Ruri tightly.

Ruri wrapped her arms around him as well. "I will be by your side forever as well, Jade-sama."

That vow was likely to be fulfilled, so long as they never doubted it.

The two slowly drew together and shared a heartfelt kiss. And then it happened. A loud crash resounded and the floors shook.

Disappointed, Jade slumped where he sat. "Well, they finally did it," he said, knowing that someone had destroyed the castle. He let Ruri off his lap and stood up. "I suppose I have no choice."

"Are you off to check?" asked Ruri.

"Yes, they'll need someone to stop any dragonkin if they're running amok."

"Tee hee hee. Being a king is hard work, isn't it?"

"It makes me want to push this job onto someone else and get back to spending my time with you."

"That would be a nice idea. Once you quit being king, then I say we build a house next to Chelsie-san's and live there together."

"That wouldn't be too bad," Jade remarked.

"In that case, let's go to Chelsie-san's place sometime and find some land where we can build a house!" Ruri said excitedly.

"I can just picture Chelsie's face now."

As they discussed their future plans, Ruri and Jade left the room hand in hand, smiles stretching across their faces.

Side Story:
A Childhood Tale

"Oho, this is you as a child, is it?" asked Jade.

"What do you think? Pretty cute, if I do say so myself," stated Ruri, tooting her own horn as she and Jade looked at a photo album that her parents had brought over from their world. They were lying in bed, shoulder to shoulder, flipping through it.

Inside were a wide variety of pictures from Ruri's childhood, dating back to when she was a newborn. With her light platinum blonde hair and younger facial features, Ruri had been as adorable as an angel. She was by no means trying to boast about herself, but she did give off that impression, objectively speaking. Then again, babies were cute regardless of their creed or country.

Ruri seemed positively delighted looking at the photos of her parents holding her in their arms. Her smile at the time made it clear that she'd had no idea that a disaster named Asahi was waiting for her down the line. If Ruri had a time machine, she would go back and plead with her parents on her hands and knees to move. That was just how perpetually cursed Ruri's life had been starting from her childhood up until she first met Chelsie. Looking at the photos, Jade caught on to that as well.

"Hm? Your hair was dark around this time," Jade said, looking at a picture of Ruri in grammar school. She was wearing a dark wig, and her face was pouty.

"That's right. That was the result of reasons beyond my control. Plus, I was already getting picked on by this point.

And even when I tried to play hooky, Asahi would come over to my house, so I couldn't run. Point is, I was pretty determined not to give in."

"I see that you had quite a rough childhood as well, Ruri," Jade commented.

Curious as to why he phrased it like that, Ruri asked, "'As well'? Were you also bullied, Jade-sama?"

That was impossible. Jade was the strongest dragonkin around—strong enough to be crowned king. There was no doubt that he'd boasted considerable strength even in his formative years.

However, contrary to Ruri's expectations, Jade confirmed his word choice with a wry smile. "Yes, I was driven to tears almost every day."

Ruri couldn't believe her ears. "Huh? Are you serious?! You're not joking?"

"I'm not. I was bullied and would come running to Master Quartz in tears," Jade admitted, smiling nostalgically.

"Wow, you had a period like that in your life?" Ruri asked, realizing that she'd never heard Jade talk about his past. "What was your childhood like, Jade-sama?"

"My childhood?"

"You said that you were driven to tears, so what kind of child were you? That was when you were with Quartz-sama, right?"

"Yes. Let's see. Well, it's hard to put into a few words, but…" Jade started as he reached back in time.

Jade was unusually weak for a dragonkin child. He was noticeably shorter than the other kids his age, and he had a mild-mannered personality. In spite of this, his mana was very strong, so much so that it would often go berserk, and he couldn't control it.

Given Jade's uniqueness, his parents had no idea what to do with him. Dragonkin, by nature, favored a hands-off approach, but with Jade's mana acting up so often, he required the tender care only parents could provide. Yet Jade's parents not only didn't cover for him, but they pretty much left him be. Dragonkin had the strength to mature even without supervision, but as Jade grew, so did his mana until finally his parents completely gave up.

It would be easy to blame his parents, but they had no idea what to do with Jade since his mana was so much stronger than their own. Dragonkin had strong bodies that could withstand their great mana, so someone whose mana went berserk, like Jade, was a rare case. After much deliberation, Jade's parents decided to leave his upbringing to Quartz, the Dragon King at the time, because he was famous for his ability to manipulate mana.

After that was decided, Jade went to live in the castle. At first, he didn't open up to anyone. Although he was just a child, the idea of being abandoned by his parents affected him to the point he became introverted. The only one who would persevere and speak to Jade was Quartz, and Jade gradually opened up to him.

One day, some kids Jade's age were bullying him, and he returned to the castle battered and bruised. Though his mana was immense and strong, his body was small and weak. There was no shortage of children who resented him for being close to the Quartz, the Dragon King. The Dragon King was the strongest entity around, the object of any child's adoration. The kids envied him because their idol took care of the weak Jade, so they constantly took out their frustrations on him.

And every time Jade came back home with tears in his eyes, Quartz would be there, greeting him with a wry smile.

"Why don't you try fighting back, Jade?" Quartz suggested.

"I can't. I mean, they come at me in numbers."

"But you can take them one-on-one?"

"That's…not possible… I'm a weakling," Jade refuted with a tear-soaked face.

"Jade, you're not weak at all."

"You can save the compliments. It makes me feel even more hollow."

"I'm not simply complimenting you. If you can master a mana as great as yours, then not only can you fight back against your bullies, but you may very well defeat me and become Dragon King yourself."

Jade gave Quartz a highly suspicious look.

"By that expression, I assume you're not convinced. All right, why don't you let me train you, then?"

"Train me?"

"The entire reason you were left in my care was so that you would learn how to handle your mana. And seeing as how you've gotten used to life in the castle, I figured that it was about time to teach you how to master your powers. Well, how about it? Care to give it a shot?"

"Will I become stronger if I train, sire?"

"But of course. I'll make you stronger than any bully."

Jade pondered it for a moment, then nodded. "I'll do it. Please train me."

"All righty, you got it. Training starts tomorrow."

After that, the grueling practice began. At first, Jade thought that Quartz was a kindly young man who always wore a gentle smile, but as soon as training started, that vision came crumbling down. With a smile that implied he wouldn't hurt a fly, Quartz conducted a gruesome regimen that brought Jade to tears every single day. No, "to tears" was putting it lightly. He bawled his eyes out.

The training was so intense that the bullying from the kids almost seemed cute. He felt ashamed of himself for crying over such meager antagonism, and he regretted ever saying that he would let Quartz teach him. He would have gladly accepted that little bit of bullying right now with a smile.

As Jade lay on the ground, a battered mess, Quartz called out to him with a jovial tone and a chipper grin.

"Come on, Jade. Quit lazing on the ground and let's have another go~!"

A demon. Quartz was a demon from the Stygian pits. Perhaps it would be better to just play dead. At this point, Jade was so utterly exhausted that he was willing to consider anything.

"If you don't get up quick, I'm adding to your regimen," Quartz said.

Jade sprung to his feet at the speed of light.

And so resumed the hellish training. It was so awful and torturous that Jade tried to run away a few times. All the same, Quartz would quickly catch him and give him even more work to do. Jade had no choice but to smarten up, let the tears flow, and face his training head-on.

Despite the pain and exhaustion, this seemed to be a blessing in disguise. Jade's mana started going berserk less often, and his body grew stronger. Granted, if he hadn't seen *any* results after working himself to the bone, Jade's heart would have probably snapped like a twig. Fortunately, he was able to feel the results, and that helped to motivate him.

One day, while Jade was going through Quartz's regimen, a number of boys walked up to him—the bullies who'd been incessantly picking on him. If he were the Jade of old, the mere look of them would have stricken him with fear, but not the Jade as he was now. The training he'd undergone was worse than *anything* they could ever dish out.

"What do you want?" Jade asked with a fierce gaze, unlike any he'd shown before.

The group of boys buckled from the pressure, but they still had their pride. They stepped forward in spite of Jade's intimidating aura.

"Y-You've got some nerve!" one of them shouted.

"About *what*?" Jade snapped back with an icy glare. It was hard to believe that this was the same Jade from not too long ago who would go crying to Quartz when he was bullied.

"You've got His Majesty taking care of a weakling like you," said the boss of the pack. "He just feels bad for you. It looks like you're getting him to train you, but there's no way that's going to make you any stronger! You're just causing His Majesty trouble!"

The boss boy took a swing at Jade. If this had been before, Jade probably would've gone flying from the punch, but now that he had trained with Quartz, he dodged the boy's hand with ease.

"Whoa!" the boy yelped—he hadn't expected Jade to evade his punch—as his momentum carried him to the ground.

The other boys were speechless.

The boss boy's face turned bright red, and he yelled at Jade to hide his embarrassment.

"What in the hell are you doing?!"

"Me? I'm not doing anything," Jade said, as if to imply that the boy had fallen on his own.

The boss boy's face got even redder. "You cocky brat!"

"Yeah, you're a cocky whelp! And a weakling!" said another boy.

"His Majesty is our idol!" another added.

Yet another chimed in, saying, "His Majesty is an incredible person. He's strong, kind, and noble."

"No. You're all being fooled," Jade replied. He'd thought the same way not too long ago—that Quartz was a very kind person. But after all of that hellish training, he wouldn't call him "kind" by any means. "That man is a *demon*. A *demonic sergeant*. Don't let his appearance fool you."

Jade didn't want to shatter their fantasy, but at the same time, he was unable to remain silent. However, only knowing Quartz from what he put on for show, none of the boys were willing to heed Jade's advice.

"That's a load of bull!"

"You dare say that after His Majesty has taken care of you?!"

"You'd better stop getting cocky. You're not his favorite just because His Majesty is kindly leading you through the basics."

"'Kindly'?" repeated Jade. He didn't think he could recover from hearing someone say that Quartz's instruction was in any way *kind*.

Jade grabbed the boss boy by the lapels. "In that case, you all can take the training too," he announced to the flock of bewildered youths.

"Whuh?" the boss boy uttered.

"I'll put the word in with Master Quartz so that all of you can be a part of the training as well."

"A-Are you serious?"

"I am," Jade said.

"And you're not lying, right? If you're lying, you're gonna get it."

"I'm not."

The boys were taken in by their own innocent, childlike glee.

"H-Hooray!"

"You mean that I can ask His Majesty to teach me?!"

Looking at them literally jumping for joy, Jade muttered under his breath, "If I'm going down, I'm taking them with me."

None of the boys noticed the sullen smile painted across Jade's face.

The following day, the boys who'd been bullying Jade up until now were standing by his side. Quartz looked at all of them, smiling as harmlessly as ever.

"There are so many of you today," he said.

"It's a pleasure, sire!" the bully boys all emphatically cried, greeting their idol.

"My regimen is mighty tough. Are you *sure* about this?" Quartz asked.

"Of course, sire. If this guy can do it, then we surely can," said the boss boy, smirking condescendingly at Jade.

The boy's smug look didn't provoke Jade at all, though. The only thing it did was evoke pity—and a tiny bit of delight.

"Since you've agreed, I will *not* let any of you off. If you want to quit, now's the time. Well?"

The boys excitedly replied, "No, sire!"

It would be interesting to see how long their energy would last.

"You're all so energetic. You'd better try to keep up, Jade."

"Yes, sire…" Jade said, his energy low.

The boys all sneered and snickered at him, but those smiles were about to vanish very soon.

Quartz looked at the boys and said, "Okay, since we have so many new faces, let's start simple today."

"No, please don't mind us; put us through the paces!" the boss boy bravely declared, perhaps trying to show off to Quartz.

Jade mentally screamed, "Stop, you fool!"

"I like your spirit," Quartz said, smiling. "In that case, I'll put you on the same regimen as Jade."

"If he can do it, then it should be cakewalk, sire."

"Is that a fact? Okay then, let me pass these out first." Quartz handed each of them the same kind of sword that Jade was currently holding.

Once the boss boy took his, he stumbled from the weight of the blade.

"Whoa, heavy!"

Everyone aside from Jade was shocked at the weight of the swords, which they were barely able to hold with both hands.

"Everyone got one? Good. Then, we'll do five thousand practice swings with those."

"Huh?"

"Huh?!"

The boys' smiles turned into grimaces.

"After that, you'll carry the swords on your back and do ten laps from Sector One to Sector Twelve as fast as you can. And then…"

"W-Wait a secon—"

"Oh, by the way, this is the morning regimen. At noon, you'll clash swords in a mock battle with real soldiers in Sector Five. In an endless rotation," Quartz said, his sweet smile looking more like a devilish smirk. At this point, everyone had already turned pale, but the training from hell wasn't over yet. "Then, after a short break, we'll buckle down with some magic control and live magic combat. I'll be the one facing you all. If you lie down or pass out, then your work for tomorrow is doubled."

Not a single trace of the bravado the boys had displayed at first remained.

"Now then, I'll be going back to work, so good luck," Quartz said before leaving.

The only ones left behind were Jade and the confused boys.

"Huh? Seriously?"

"That was a *joke*, right?"

"W-Well, duh, of course it was…"

As the boys half-heartedly laughed, Jade grumbled, "Hey, what are you all doing? Morning will be over unless you hurry up."

"Huh?"

"Just to let you know, if you don't finish before morning is up, then you'll get double the amount of work tomorrow."

Seeing how serious Jade looked as he said that, the boys finally understood that this was no joke. They began to panic when they saw Jade start swinging his sword, but they couldn't seem to swing their own massive swords—weapons so girthy that even dragonkin children had to hold them with both hands. Meanwhile, Jade was swinging his sword just fine, albeit miserably.

One of the boys who noticed this launched a complaint. "Hey, lend me your sword. Yours is lighter, isn't it?"

Jade silently handed his sword to the boy, but the sheer weight of it caused the boy to relinquish the weapon. The sword hit the ground with an abnormally loud thud, causing the other boys to gather around.

"That's a heck of a sound. Hey, you try holding it," said one of the boys.

"Sure, I'll just… What the…? This is crazy heavy!"

"This is heavier than ours!"

All eyes turned to Jade.

"You've been swinging this thing around?" the boss boy asked.

"I have," Jade replied.

It was clear that their impressions of Jade had changed ever so slightly.

In the end, the boys couldn't do the morning routine half as well as Jade could. After lunch, they all had live combat practice against real soldiers in Sector Five's training grounds, followed by Quartz's magic training. Then, after *all that* was over, the regimen from hell left a pile of exhausted bodies in its wake.

"Oh, since no one aside from Jade was able to complete the regimen, you get double tomorrow," Quartz said. His words were the kiss of death to the other boys' morale.

Out of all the boys, Jade was the quickest to recover because he had the most experience. He slowly stood up and said, "Now do you understand? I told you. Master Quartz is *not* a kind person by any stretch."

No one had enough stamina left to even reply to Jade's remark.

"And that was how my youth went," Jade finished.

"Mm-hmm. I'm not sure how to put this. Quartz-sama is surprisingly strict—'Spartan,' as they say in my language. Any human would've been dead by now."

"Indeed. I've never been so glad to be a dragonkin than in that period of my life. I recovered from wounds fast as well," Jade said, his voice deep as he remembered those days.

"So, tell me, whatever happened to the boys who used to pick on you, Jade-sama?"

"At first, we squabbled, but the training was so severe that bullying anyone became the furthest thing from their minds. Ever since that day, they have completely stopped. In fact, we actually bonded as comrades facing a powerful enemy. Nowadays, we're drinking buddies."

"Wow, you all sure got chummy, then," Ruri commented.

"Because we had a huge wall to overcome named Master Quartz. It was truly severe. And I mean that…" Jade said with a somewhat distant look in his eyes.

Those experiences sounded like they'd been *very* rough—something Ruri couldn't envision based on her perception of Quartz.

"Back then, we'd often joke about someone from our group taking Master Quartz down and becoming king to show him up."

"And that ended up happening since you became king, right?"

"Well, I actually didn't fight Master Quartz at all, and I couldn't believe that I became king in the first place. Still, all of the boys I trained with were happy for me, even more so than me."

Jade smiled nostalgically. Ruri couldn't help but giggle, seeing him act like that.

"Ruri?" Jade questioned.

"Oh, no. It's just that I'm marveling at how you, of all people, spent your younger days."

"Don't treat me like some old man. I'm young for a dragonkin."

Ruri knew that Jade would be pushing past his twilight years if he were human, but she decided not to mention it aloud.

"It's good that you have people like that, though. Comrades you spent your childhood with, that is. I never had any friends like that, so it makes me envious."

Ruri had never had any close friends—none that she could call a "comrade" or a "bosom buddy," anyway—since Asahi would constantly get in the way. One could say that this was the very reason Ruri was so quick to adapt to this world, even though she knew she could never return to her own. She probably would have made more of a fuss if all her loved ones had remained in her world and never came here, so in that respect, it was likely a good thing that she'd never had anyone especially close to her. Nonetheless, hearing a story like Jade's was bound to make her feel a tinge of envy.

"You have Celestine, don't you?" Jade offered.

Ruri choked on her words. "Let's just say I'm pretty hesitant about whether I should put Celestine-san in the 'friend' category..."

"In my eyes, you two look to get along just fine, so why not?"

"Hmm… I mean, I don't *dislike* her. I actually think that she's an interesting individual. It's just that… A friend? Well…"

A part of Ruri didn't want to recognize Celestine as a friend. After all, Celestine had yet to give up on Jade. If it weren't for that one thing, they probably could have built a good relationship, just as Jade said, but Ruri felt that it was still too early for them. Perhaps Celestine would give up in another ten years? Perhaps when Ruri and Jade had a child? No, Ruri's instincts told her that something so minor would not deter Celestine.

"Yeah, I don't think that'll be happening for a while," Ruri admitted, assuming that Celestine would give the same answer if posed with the same question. Ruri and Celestine were rivals in love, at least for now.

"So I see," replied Jade, chuckling.

"Do you still interact with those people, Jade-sama?"

"Yes. In fact, they're all soldiers at the castle."

"Huh?!" Ruri gasped, surprised. She pretty much knew every dragonkin soldier in the castle. That meant that the bullies who'd tormented Jade in the past would have to be among them. "Do I know any of them?" she asked.

"I'd assume you would at least recognize their faces. You're always going off to the training grounds in Sector Five, and they're always on guard duty or patrol in Sector One."

"Huh, I wonder which of them it is. Maybe I'll ask around when I have a chance."

"I don't think they'll answer you even if you ask. They *do* have a dishonorable record of bullying the Dragon King."

"Jade-sama, you're making an *extremely* devious expression, you know," Ruri said, commenting on his smirk.

"Sometimes I tease those lugs about it, and they get shaken up in the funniest ways."

"Yes, I bet they would."

The children back then would've had no way of knowing that the boy they were bullying would turn out to be the very Dragon King they so idolized. Certainly, that piece of their past was a dark history they carried to this day, and Jade toying with them about it probably did a number on their hearts. Considering that, Jade was behaving just as stellar as they once had. To be fair, though, it *was* a cheeky little way of getting payback for what had happened in the past.

"Do you want me to take you to see them?" Jade asked.

"Yes. That would be great!" Ruri answered immediately, genuinely curious about the people who shared moments of Jade's precious childhood.

"I can't wait to see the look on those buncha lugs' faces. They seemed to be smitten with you when you were a fluffy little cat too. I bet the hope will leave their eyes once they find out you know about what they did to me back then," Jade said, making an evil face yet again.

That was when it hit Ruri. Jade was speaking demonstrably more colloquially.

"Jade-sama? You have a different personality when you speak about your friends, don't you?" Ruri asked.

"Do I?" Jade replied with a blank stare, seemingly clueless to the fact himself.

"You do. Your speech is more…childish? Or perhaps casual. I can more or less tell that you open yourself up to those people."

"Is that how I seem?"

"Yes, and as your *wife*, I'm a tad jealous, I must say," Ruri declared, making a deliberately sulky face.

215

Jade laughed and said, "We went through *a lot* in the past, but they're friends near and dear to me now. Still…" Jade trailed off, suddenly bringing his face to Ruri's and lightly pecking her on the lips, "it goes without saying that *you* mean the most to me, Ruri."

"I'm relieved to hear that," Ruri said with a satisfied smile, glad to hear it although she'd never doubted it in the first place.

"I can set up a meeting, but there will be no turning into a cat and letting them pet you," Jade decreed.

"No one has touched me since we've gotten married, Jade-sama, out of respect for you."

Dragonkin knew better than anyone how much they cherished their mates and how jealous they became. Maybe that was the reason, when she'd traversed the castle in cat form in the past, that people came out of nowhere to pat her on the head and left. Ever since the wedding, though, no one would come up to touch her even if she *was* out and about in cat form. She could feel resentful gazes from afar, but that was it. Now that she had become a proper mate, not a single soul could touch her.

Ruri would often hear the sad screams of the dragonkin pointing out her fluffiness or lamenting never being able to experience her soft body ever again. However, there was nothing that Ruri could do, other than tell them to give up. Jade had said that they were smitten with her in cat form, so it was possible that his friends were among those people.

"In that case, maybe I should really lay it on thick and pet your fluffy body in front of them. That'd be a good way to harass 'em."

"Jade-sama, you really *do* switch personalities when you talk about them."

Jade would act differently with Quartz than he would with others, but this was even more pronounced than that. He was acting *maliciously*.

It made Ruri look forward to seeing how he interacted with them once they met in person. She was sure that she would discover some new facet of Jade she never knew.

"Of course, they *are* great friends of mine," Jade replied with a smile as kind as could be.

VII

VOL. 7
ON SALE NOW!

Tearmoon Empire

Nozomu Mochitsuki
Illustrator: Gilse

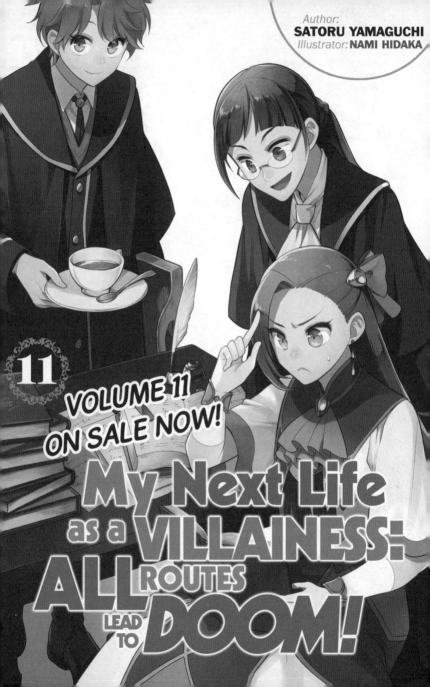

2

COMPLETE SERIES
ON SALE NOW!

Author: **Ameko Kaeruda**
Illustrator: **Kazutomo Miya**

SEXILED

My Sexist Party Leader Kicked Me Out,
So I Teamed Up With a Mythical Sorceress

Bibliophile Princess

Novel + Manga
Available from
All Major
Ebook Stores

Author: Yui
Illustrator: Satsuki Sheena

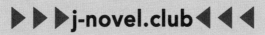

J-Novel Club Lineup

Latest Ebook Releases Series List